APOCRYPHA

IMMORTAL SHE-HULK

AL EWING
WRITER

N DAVIS-HUNT
ARTIST

ARCIO MENYZ
COLOR ARTIST

S CORY PETIT
LETTERER

JOE BENNETT, RUY JOSÉ & PAUL MOUNTS
COVER ART

RAH BRUNSTAD
ASSOCIATE EDITOR

WIL MOSS
EDITOR

KING IN BLACK: IMMORTAL HULK

AL EWING
WRITER

AARON KUDER
ARTIST

FRANK MARTIN & ERICK ARCINIEGA
COLOR ARTISTS

VC's CORY PETIT
LETTERER

AARON KUDER & FRANK MARTIN
COVER ART

SARAH BRUNSTAD
ASSOCIATE EDITOR

WIL MOSS
EDITOR

IMMORTAL HULK: TIME OF THE MONSTERS

ALEX PAKNADEL & AL EWING
STORY

ALEX PAKNADEL
SCRIPT

JUAN FERREYRA
ARTIST

VC's CORY PETIT
LETTERER

JUAN FERREYRA
COVER ART

SPECIAL THANKS TO PROFESSOR NATALIE MUNRO & DR. STEPHEN CURTIS

WIL MOSS & SARAH BRUNSTAD
EDITORS

HULK CREATED BY STAN LEE & JACK KIRBY

JENNIFER GRÜNWALD
COLLECTION EDITOR

DANIEL KIRCHHOFFER
ASSISTANT EDITOR

MAIA LOY
ASSISTANT MANAGING EDITOR

LISA MONTALBANO
ASSISTANT MANAGING EDITOR

JEFF YOUNGQUIST
VP PRODUCTION & SPECIAL PROJECTS

DAVID GABRIEL
SVP PRINT, SALES & MARKETING

C.B. CEBULSKI
EDITOR IN CHIEF

MMORTAL HULK VOL. 11: APOCRYPHA. Contains material originally published in magazine form as IMMORTAL HULK: THE BES … E CARNAGE: MMORTAL HULK (2019) #1, IMMORTAL HULK (2020) #0, IMMORTAL SHE-HULK (2020) #1, KING IN BLACK: IMMORTAL HULK (2020 … ISBN 978-1-02-93116-2. Published by MARVEL WORLDWIDE, INC., a subsidiary of MARVEL ENTERTAINMENT, LLC. OFFICE OF PUBLICATION: … arity between ny of the names, characters, persons, and/or institutions in this book with those of any living or dead person or institution is in … **d in Canada.** KEVIN FEIGE, Chief Creative Officer; DAN BUCKLEY, President, Marvel Entertainment; JOE QUESADA, EVP & Creative Director; DAV … cutive Editor; NICK LOWE, Executive Editor, VP of Content, Digital Publishing; DAVID GABRIEL, VP of Print & Digital Publishing; JEFF YOUNGQU … g Operations; DAN EDINGTON, Managing Editor; RICKEY PURDIN, Director of Talent Relations; JENNIFER GRÜNWALD, Senior Editor, Special Pr … or information regarding advertising in Marvel Comics or on Marvel.com, please contact Vit DeBellis, Custom Solutions & Integrated Advertising … call 888-511-5480. **Manufactured between 10/29/2021 and 11/30/2021 by SOLISCO PRINTERS, SCOTT, QC, CANADA.**

ADI GRANOV
IMMORTAL HULK: THE BEST DEFENSE VARIANT

SKOTTIE YOUNG
IMMORTAL HULK: THE BEST DEFENSE VARIANT

OE BENNETT, BELARDINO BRABO & PAUL MOUNTS
IMMORTAL HULK: THE BEST DEFENSE VARIANT

JACK KIRBY & PAUL MOUNTS
IMMORTAL HULK: THE BEST DEFENSE HIDDEN GEM VARIANT

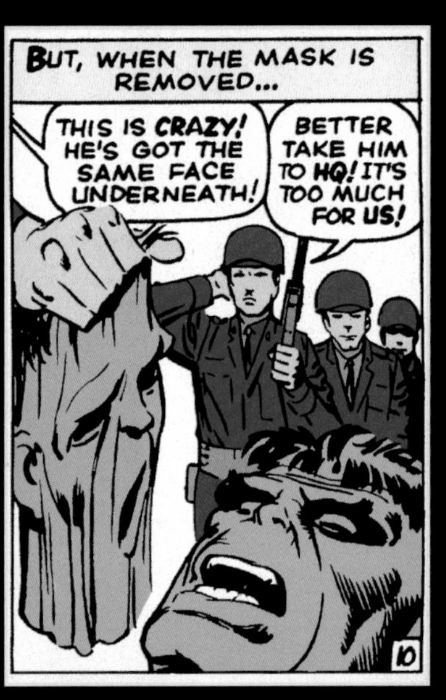
BUT, WHEN THE MASK IS REMOVED...
THIS IS CRAZY! HE'S GOT THE SAME FACE UNDERNEATH!
BETTER TAKE HIM TO HQ! IT'S TOO MUCH FOR US!
10

SOMEWHERE IN NEW MEXICO.
MY NAME IS BRUCE BANNER.
I GOT THE HUNCH HALF AN HOUR AGO.

I'M THE RATIONAL ONE, YOU SEE. THE SCIENTIST. I BELIEVE IN WHAT I PERCEIVE WITH MY FIVE SENSES.
HUNCHES, GUT FEELINGS, MAGICAL THINKING-- THAT'S THE REPRESSED, IRRATIONAL SIDE.

THAT'S HIM TALKING TO ME.
THE OTHER GUY.

THAT BRUTAL, BESTIAL MOCKERY OF A HUMAN--THAT CREATURE WHICH FEARS NOTHING--WHICH DESPISES REASON AND WORSHIPS POWER!

AN ITCH IN MY SKULL LIKE A HOMING BEACON. A COMPASS, TELLING ME WHERE TO GO.
HE KNOWS THERE'S SOMETHING HERE...

AH.
A NAME POPS INTO MY HEAD.
"STEVE."

HIS NAME FOR DR. STEPHEN STRANGE.
THE MAN WHO'S LYING IN FRONT OF ME.

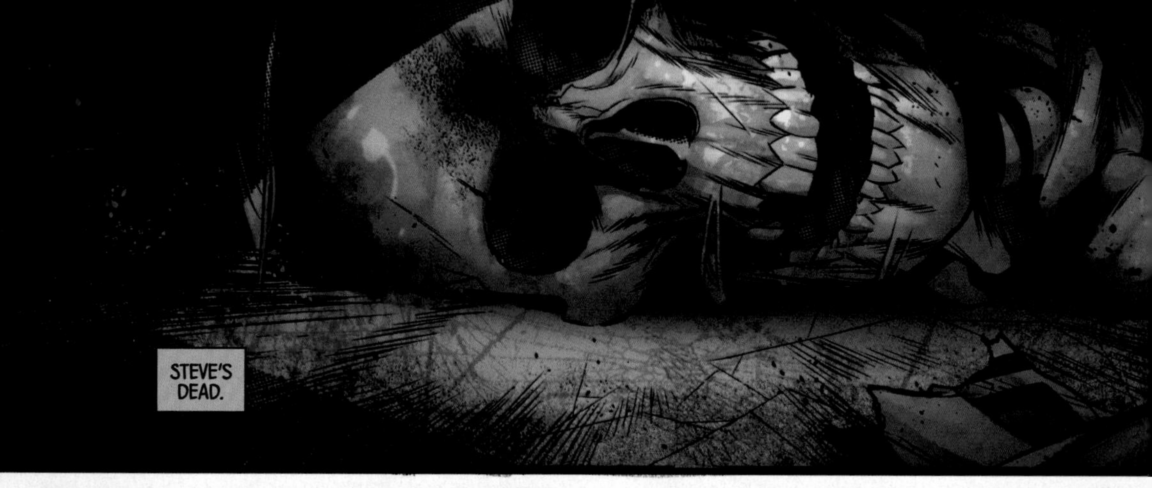
STEVE'S DEAD.

THE FACE UNDERNEATH

AL EWING WRITER SIMONE DI MEO ARTIST DONO SÁNCHEZ-ALMARA COLORIST
VC'S CORY PETIT LETTERER RON GARNEY & RICHARD ISANOVE COVER
JOE BENNETT, BELARDINO BRABO & PAUL MOUNTS; ADI GRANOV; JACK KIRBY & PAUL MOUNTS; SKOTTIE YOUNG VARIANT COVER ARTISTS
AL EWING, CHIP ZDARSKY, JASON LATOUR & GERRY DUGGAN DEFENDERS MASTERMINDS
ALANNA SMITH ASSOCIATE EDITOR TOM BREVOORT EDITOR
C.B. CEBULSKI EDITOR IN CHIEF JOE QUESADA CHIEF CREATIVE OFFICER DAN BUCKLEY PRESIDENT ALAN FINE EXECUTIVE PRODUCER
REPRINT PANELS FROM INCREDIBLE HULK VOL.1 #1-3 & #6 BY STAN LEE, JACK KIRBY, STEVE DITKO, PAUL REINMAN, DICK AYERS & ART SIMEK
HULK CREATED BY STAN LEE & JACK KIRBY

IT'S DEFINITELY HIM.
HE'S BEEN BURNED TO THE BONE... AND SOMETHING'S MISSING FROM THE BODY.
THE AMULET HE ALWAYS WORE-- IT'S NOT HERE.
THE EYE OF SOMETHING... AGAMEMNON...
...THE EYE OF AGAMOTTO.
DOCTOR STRANGE'S TALISMAN. IT SAW THE TRUTH LOCKED INSIDE PEOPLE. IT COULD TEAR OUT WHAT WAS HIDDEN...
...AND THAT'S MORE THAN MOTIVE ENOUGH FOR MURDER.
STEVE AND I HAD OUR DISAGREEMENTS. SOMETIMES VIOLENT ONES.
BUT HE ALWAYS LET ME STAY AT HIS HOUSE-- AND THAT'S NO SMALL THING TO A MAN WITHOUT A HOME.
STEVE...WAS A FRIEND OF MINE.
AND SOMEONE KILLED HIM OVER A FIST-SIZED CHUNK OF METAL.
THAT MAKES ME ANGRY.

THE TIMING ISN'T GREAT.
NIGHT IS THE HULK'S TIME--BUT RIGHT NOW, IT'S JUST PAST NOON. HE WON'T BE APPEARING IN PERSON.

AND MAYBE THAT'S FOR THE BEST. SOMETHING'S GOTTEN INTO HIM. INTO US.
I DON'T KNOW THE FULL STORY--WE DON'T TALK TO EACH OTHER THE WAY WE USED TO--BUT UNTIL WE CURE OUR... INFECTION...

...WE JUST CAN'T TRUST OURSELVES.
SO I'M NOT LETTING YOU OUT, HULK.
FAIR?

HMM.

NO ANSWERING ITCH IN MY SKULL. NO STRANGE HUNCHES OR COMPULSIONS...

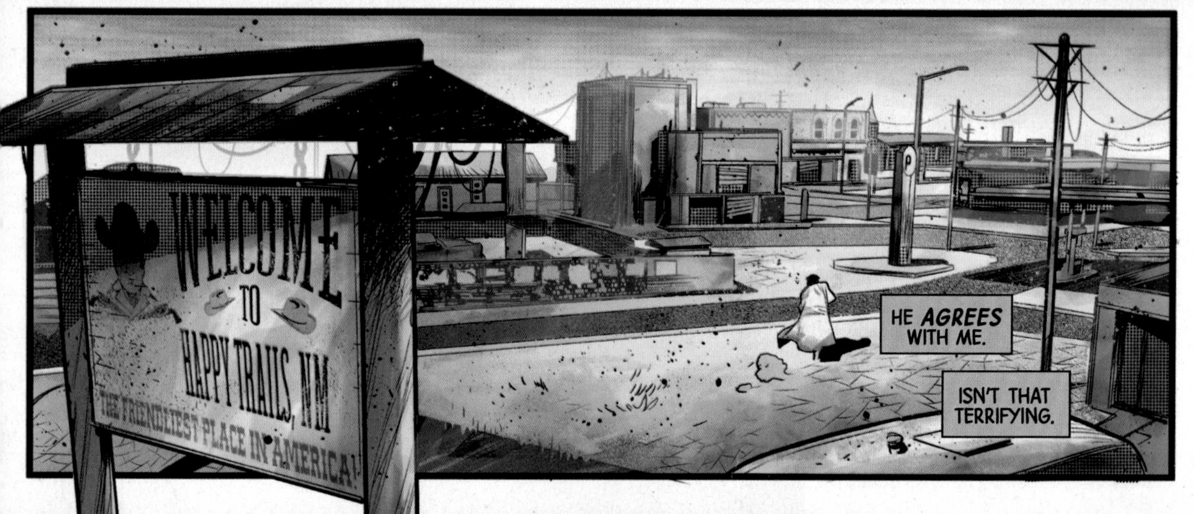

WELCOME TO HAPPY TRAILS, NM
THE FRIENDLIEST PLACE IN AMERICA!
HE AGREES WITH ME.
ISN'T THAT TERRIFYING.

HAPPY TRAILS
MARSHAL'S OFFICE
ALL RIGHT. WE'RE NOT IN A POSITION TO DEAL WITH THIS ONE. I ACCEPT THAT.
THE LOCAL POLICE, THEN. I'LL POINT THEM IN THE RIGHT DIRECTION, THEN SLIP AWAY.

THEY'LL CALL STARK OR DANVERS. SOMEONE QUALIFIED TO DO THE RIGHT THING FOR STEPHEN.
THE HEROES CAN SOLVE THE MURDER AND SAVE THE DAY, AND IT'LL BE LIKE I WAS NEVER...

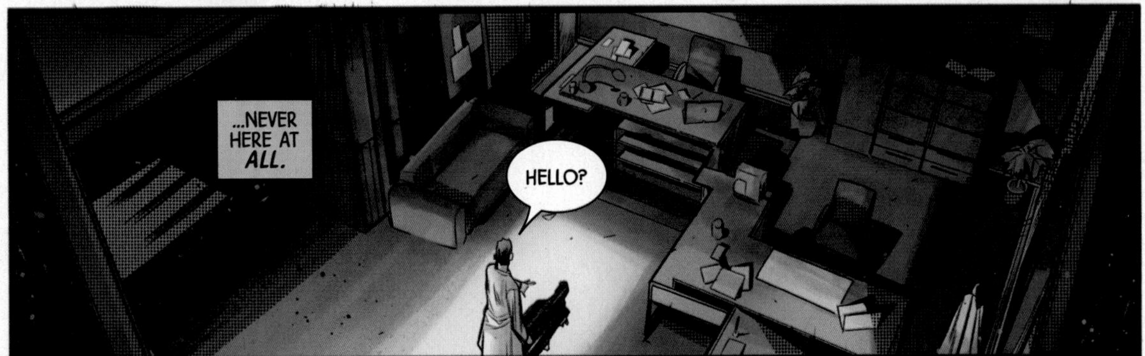
...NEVER HERE AT ALL.
HELLO?

LET'S NOT JUMP TO CONCLUSIONS, BRUCE.

HELLO?
ANYONE?
I'M SURE THERE'S A GOOD EXPLANATION FOR A TOTALLY EMPTY POLICE STATION IN THE MIDDLE OF THE DAY...

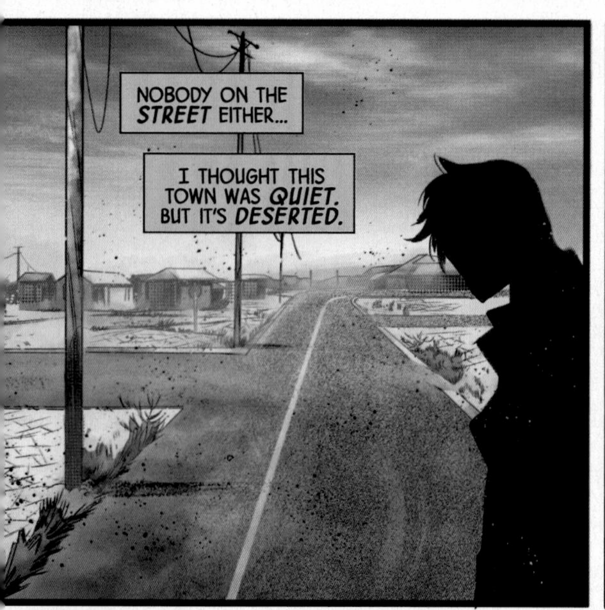
NOBODY ON THE STREET EITHER...
I THOUGHT THIS TOWN WAS QUIET. BUT IT'S DESERTED.

I'D GET SOME ANSWERS AT THE BAR--MY USUAL METHOD IN A STRANGE TOWN--

--BUT IT'S CLOSED RIGHT NOW.
AND FOREVER, BY THE LOOK OF IT.
RAWHIDE SALOON
CLOSED

SO WHAT ARE WE LOOKING AT? A GHOST TOWN? BUT THERE ARE STILL CARS AND TRUCKS HERE...
CARS...AND TRUCKS...

...AND TWITCHY CURTAINS...

...AND PEOPLE.

ALL RIGHT.
LET'S GET SOME ANSWERS.
EXCUSE ME?

HELLO?
CAN I COME IN, PLEASE? I WON'T TAKE UP MUCH OF YOUR TIME--

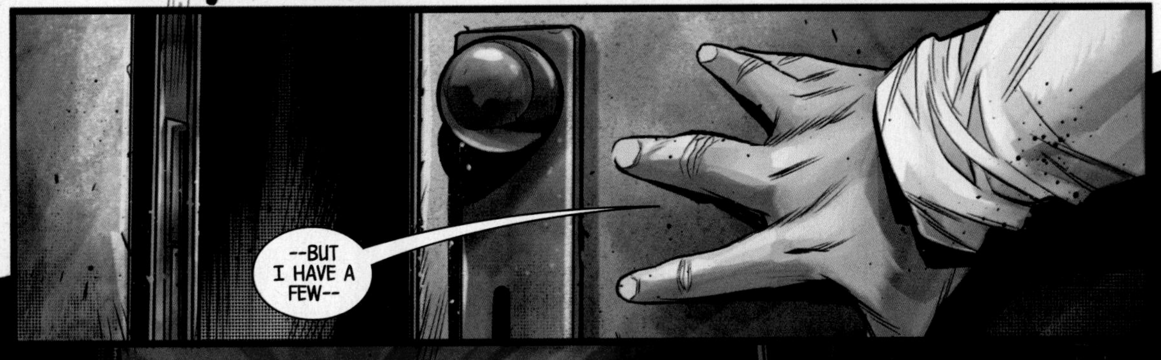
--BUT I HAVE A FEW--

--QUESTIONS.
PAUSE.

INTERLUDE.
<WHAT WAS THAT NOISE...?>*
*TRANSLATED FROM A MINOR RIMWORLD DIALECT.

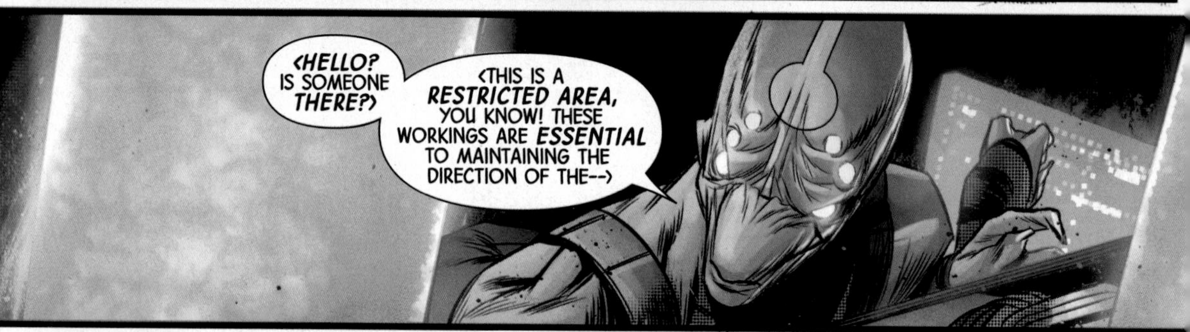
<HELLO? IS SOMEONE THERE?>
<THIS IS A RESTRICTED AREA, YOU KNOW! THESE WORKINGS ARE ESSENTIAL TO MAINTAINING THE DIRECTION OF THE-->

BOO!

HEE HEE HEE
INTERLUDE COMPLETE.

RESUME.
WE DON'T WANT TROUBLE.
HE--HE DOESN'T KNOW I'M HERE.

AND YOU DON'T WANT TO BE HERE EITHER.
YOU DON'T. JUST--JUST TURN AROUND, MISTER.

JUST GO.

GET OUT OF MY WAY, INSECT!

GET OUT
OF
MY

WAY--
HNHH--
NO! STAY BACK!! DON'T-- DON'T!!
YOU WILL SHOOT ME NO MORE!

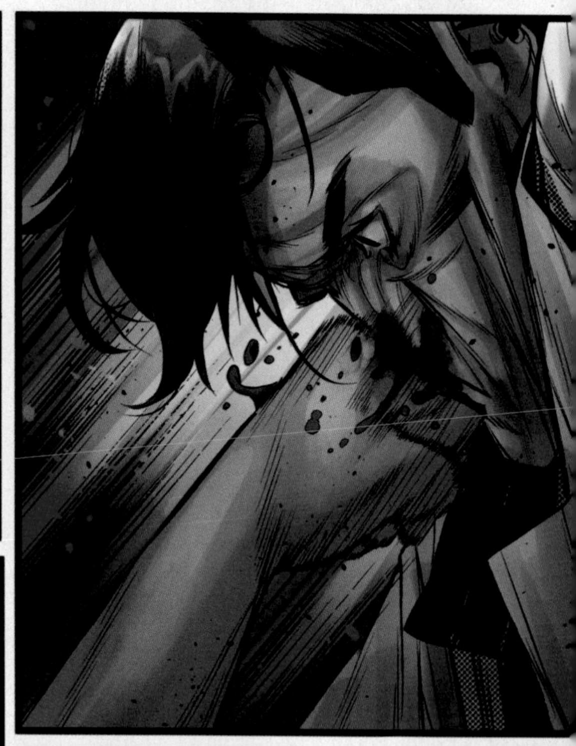

YOU DARE ATTACK THE HULK??!

AAH--

AAAHH--

GET--GET OUT--

GET OUT! GET OUT!

WHY ARE YOU HERE? WHY?

WHY ARE YOU HERE?

HATE YOU?? WHY SHOULDN'T I HATE YOU? WHY SHOULDN'T I HATE ALL MANKIND??

HRRHH--

--AAHH!

MY EYE--

ARGHHH!

LITTLE PSYCHO--

YEAH? YOU LIKE THAT?
YOU LIKE THAT?

BIH
BIH MUH

TUNG

NOW-- REVENGE!!!
NO! NO!

STOP IT!
STOP IT!

HFFF.
HHH.
HHUH. NUH.
SO! THIS IS WHAT THE PUNY HUMANS FEAR!
NUH.
NOBODY AROUND. WANT TO KNOW WHY.
TALK NOW.

HORP
OKAY.
OKAY.
OKAY.
RAWHIDE SALOON
MY USUAL METHOD.
CLOSED

KNOCK, KNOCK.

WHO'S--
THERE--
CLOSED

HNNGH--

OUT!!

OPEN--
YOU--

RRRH--

NO.
I'M THE MAN WHO SEES *YOU.*

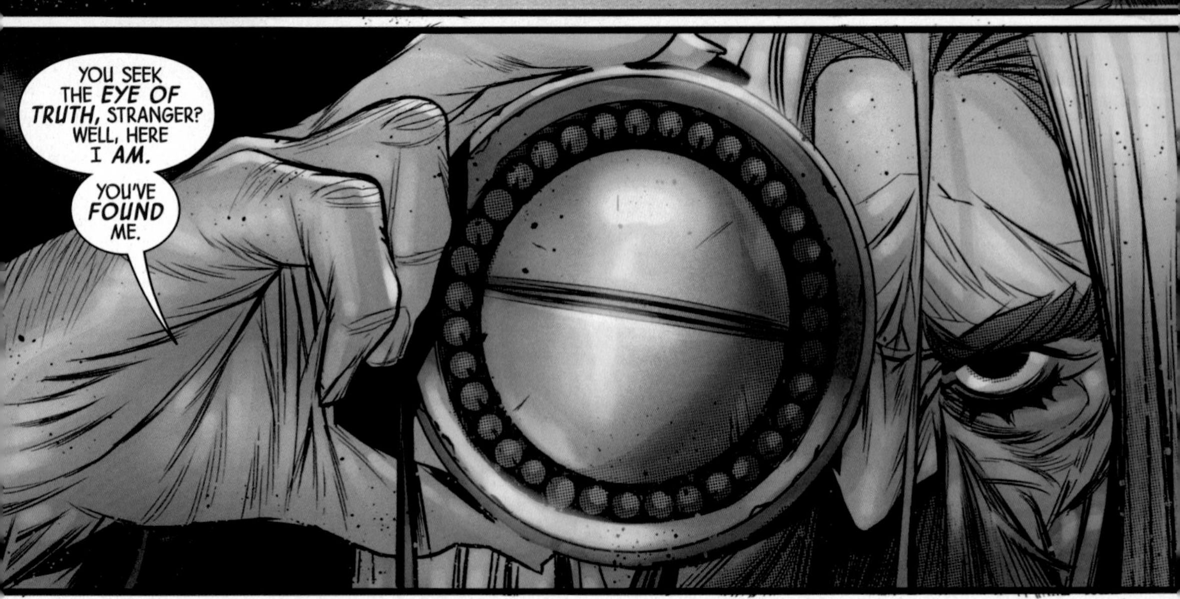

HMH.
OVER THERE. THAT'S NOT A MAGIC *SPELL,* IS IT?

YOU JUST TOLD THEM *NOT TO MOVE.* AND THEY *DIDN'T.*
FOR...*HOW* LONG? HOURS? A *DAY?* MUSCLES *CRAMPING,* HOLDING IN THEIR BLADDERS... OR *NOT.* I CAN SMELL *URINE.*
BUT THEY DON'T MOVE.

BECAUSE THE ALTERNATIVE... WOULD BE *WORSE.*

HEH.

YOU KNOW... I UNDERSTAND SOMETHING ABOUT *REVENGE,* MISTER EYE.
TELL ME WHAT THEY *DID.*

"THEY SAID I DESERVED IT.

"VAGRANCY. DISTURBING THE PEACE.
"SIMPLY EXISTING."

I WAS SOMETHING THEY DIDN'T WANT TO SEE, YOU SEE.
AN UNPLEASANT TRUTH.

"SO THEY BEAT ME BLOODY AND DUMPED ME AT THE EDGE OF TOWN. CAST ME OUT INTO THE NIGHT.

"IT WAS COLD. I WAS ALONE. BLEEDING...FREEZING...
"BUT THERE WAS A BARN...

"...AND IN THE BARN WAS A MAGIC FIRE, CAST BY A MAGIC MAN..."

SO HE WAS ALREADY BURNING? HE WAS DEAD WHEN YOU FOUND HIM?
THAT DETAIL'S IMPORTANT.
OH, YES. HE WAS DEAD...

"...AND HIS EYE WAS OPEN.
"WHEN IT LOOKED INTO ME, IT SHOWED ME THE SECRET TRUTH... THE TRUTH OF MYSELF...

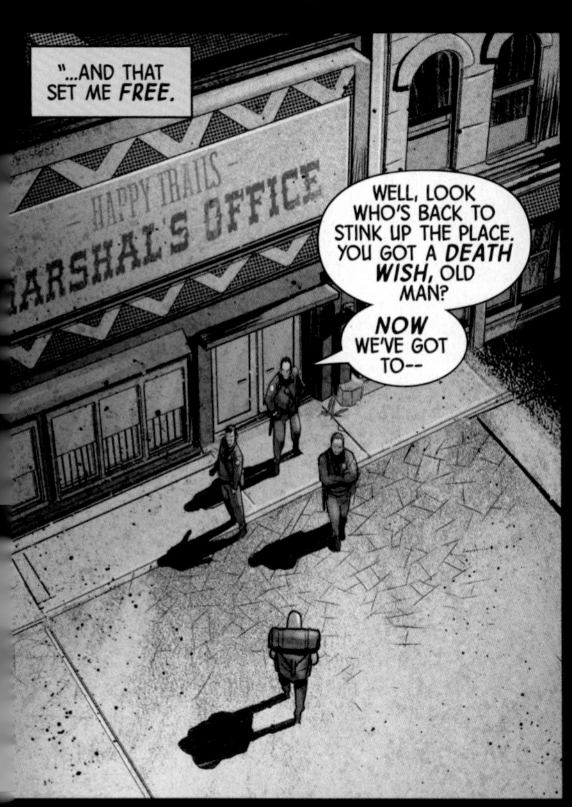
"...AND THAT SET ME FREE.
HAPPY TRAILS
MARSHAL'S OFFICE
WELL, LOOK WHO'S BACK TO STINK UP THE PLACE. YOU GOT A DEATH WISH, OLD MAN?
NOW WE'VE GOT TO--

"FREE TO SHOW OTHERS THEIR TRUTH."
LOOK INTO MY EYE.
LOOK AT YOURSELVES.

N-NO! STOP IT!
MAKE IT STOP!

THE TRUTH OF WHO THEY TRULY *ARE.* THEIR OWN *SOULS,* IN DETAIL RESERVED FOR THE EYE OF GOD *HIMSELF.*
WOULD YOU LIKE TO SEE YOURSELF *AGAIN,* MARSHAL? IN ALL YOUR *MAJESTY* AND *GLORY?*
NO.
NO, SIR.
PLEASE.
...
ALL RIGHT.
I *DO* UNDERSTAND REVENGE, BUT...YOU'VE *HAD* YOURS. AND I DON'T THINK MY *FRIEND* WOULD LIKE THE WAY YOU'RE USING HIS *TOOLS.*
GIVE.
BUT YOUR *FRIEND* ISN'T *HERE.*
FAIR WARNING, STRANGER. YOU DON'T WANT MY EYE LOOKING AT *YOU--*
WELL...WHY *NOT?*
LET'S TRY IT.

WHAT...?

COME ON. THAT'S A ***MAGIC*** THING, AFTER ALL. IT BREAKS THE ***RULES.***

LET'S SEE IF IT BRINGS OUT ***MY*** HIDDEN TRUTH.

NO.

I'VE CHANGED MY MIND.

OH?

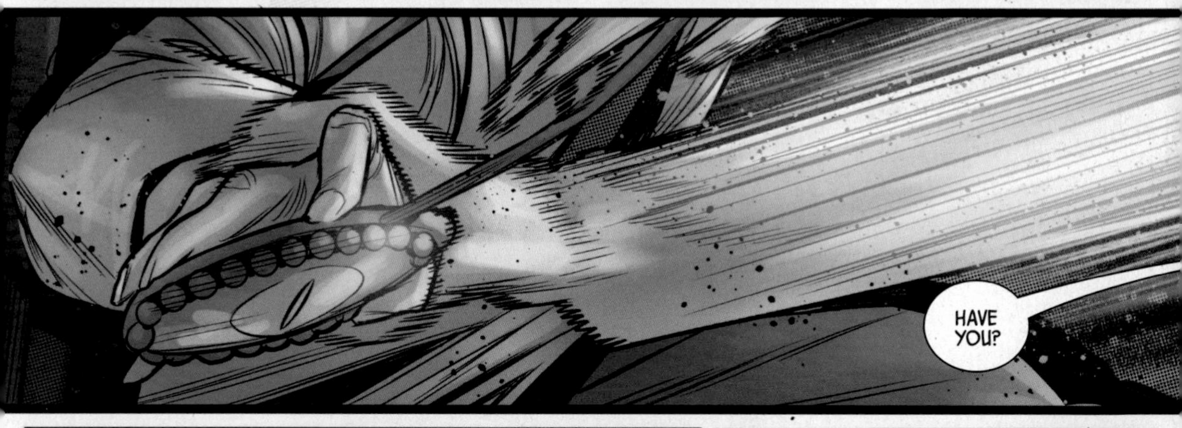
HAVE YOU?

GIVE IT ***HERE--***
GET ***BACK!*** LET GO!
MARSHAL! GET HIM ***OFF*** ME!

I--I--
DO IT!
DO AS YOU'RE TOLD!

IS--IS THAT--
AGAIN! IN THE HEAD!
DO IT!

YOU WANT ME TO KILL HIM?

NOW YOU TASTE THE STING OF YOUR WEAPON!

I--I CAN'T JUST--
LOOK OUT--

AAAHH!

AH-AH-AH.
BACK AWAY.

REMEMBER. THIS...THIS IS WHAT YOU WANT.
DON'T MAKE ME ANGRY.

G-GET HIM! STOP HIM!
HERE'S AN AGE-OLD TRUTH, MISTER EYE...

...QUIT WHILE YOU'RE AHEAD.
AAHH--

AND NOW...
KNOCK, KNOCK.

HNH.
WHO'S THERE?

...
YOU KNOW I'M A LOT BETTER THAN BANNER IN A FIGHT, RIGHT?

JUST THE TWO OF US, THEN.

WE CAN MAKE IT IF WE TRY.
DON'T-- PLEASE-- DON'T HURT ME--
I JUST WANTED TO-- TO MAKE THEM PAY--

NEVER STOP MAKING THEM PAY. LIKE BANNER SAID--WE'RE REAL UNDERSTANDING ABOUT THAT.
FOR INSTANCE, IF SOMEONE HURTS HIM...I TAKE IT PERSONAL.

YOU GOT HIM SHOT, BEATEN AND HIT WITH A NIGHTSTICK. THAT HURT A LOT.
AND NOW I'M OUT IN THE DAY. THAT'S NO PICNIC EITHER.
SO.

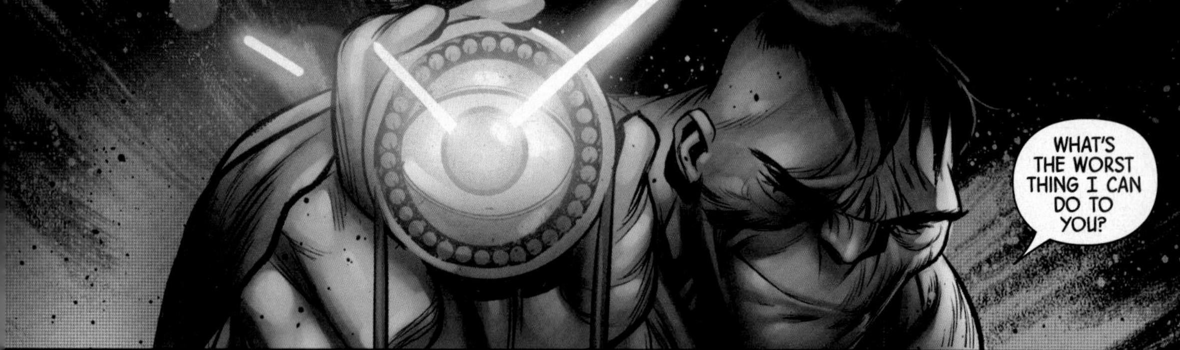
WHAT'S THE WORST THING I CAN DO TO YOU?

NO! STOP! STOP IT!
STOP LOOKING AT ME!
LIKE I THOUGHT.

EVEN INSIDE BANNER, I KNEW YOU WERE LYING ABOUT THAT PART. THE TRUTH DIDN'T SET YOU FREE--IT JUST TORTURED YOU.
NICE WEAPON TO THREATEN THE OTHER PUNY HUMANS WITH, THOUGH.

NOBODY LIKES THE FACE UNDERNEATH...
JUST-- JUST LET ME GO. PLEASE.
I DIDN'T KILL YOUR FRIEND-- I WASN'T LYING ABOUT THAT--

THAT'S WHY YOU'RE BREATHING. I SOLVED THAT MURDER MYSTERY BEFORE BANNER EVEN SAW THE BODY.
WHO KILLED STEPHEN STRANGE?

YOU DID.
WHO...?
AM I RIGHT?

WELL, HULK...
...THEREBY HANGS A *TALE.*

THIS IS THE TRAIN.
YOU'VE SEEN IT ON THE EDGE OF SLEEPLESS NIGHTS. YOU KNOW IT WELL.
THE GREAT ENGINE OF PLANETS. A JUGGERNAUT OF LIVING WORLDS, HURTLING HEADLONG THROUGH SPACE.
IT PULLS IN NEW WORLDS ALONG THE WAY, TAKES EVERYTHING OF THEM THAT'S THEIR OWN AND--WHEN IT'S DRAINED THEM DRY--IT MAKES FUEL OF THEM IN ITS FURNACE.
IF THEY RESIST, KEEP WHAT'S THEIRS, WHAT'S IMPORTANT--THEY END UP AS FUEL ANYWAY. IN THE END, EVERYTHING WILL BE FUEL FOR THE TRAIN.
IT'D MAKE AN EXCELLENT METAPHOR IF IT WEREN'T REAL.
THE THRONE, THE POWER, THE DAMNED AND THE DEVIL
Writer: Al Ewing
Penciler: Joe Bennett
Inker: Belardino Brabo
Color Artist: Dono Sánchez-Almara
Letterer: VC's Clayton Cowles

THIS IS THE CONDUCTOR. THE ONE WHO DRIVES THE TRAIN.
IT DIRECTS THE PLANETS INTO THE FURNACE, AS IT HAS SINCE BEFORE THE FIRST MEMORY. ITS LABOR IS ENDLESS.
MAYBE THAT'S A METAPHOR AS WELL. WHO CAN SAY? I STUDIED MEDICINE, NOT POETRY--THOUGH I'VE FOUND SOME POETRY IN EXISTENCE SINCE.
THE CONDUCTOR WORKS ON, THOUGH ITS WILL IS NO LONGER ITS OWN.
THERE IS SOMETHING COILED AROUND ITS MIND.

THIS IS A *DEAD THING.*
UNTIL RECENTLY, IT WAS MOVING FROM WORLD TO WORLD IN A MORE *HUMANOID* FORM, MURDERING THE CONDUCTOR'S *FAMILIARS*--ITS MORTAL SERVANTS AND FACILITATORS.
THAT WAS TO GET A CLEAR RUN AT THE CONDUCTOR *ITSELF.* NOW THIS DEAD THING--THIS ALIEN *GHOST*--COMMANDS THE TRAIN AND SETS IT ON ITS COURSE.
I *KNEW* IT, WHEN IT WAS ALIVE.
IT HAD A *NAME.*
NEBULON...

...DO YOU REMEMBER ME?
THIS ONE WIELDS A POWER INCONCEIVABLE TO MAN. HE HAD A NAME ONCE, TOO--NORRIN RADD.
NOW...HE IS THE SILVER SURFER.
...
YES, NORRIN RADD.
I DO.
GOOD. BECAUSE I REMEMBER YOU, NEBULON.
AN ALIEN PROSPECTOR, TURNED CULT LEADER, TURNED TRAITOR TO HIS SPECIES...
...TURNED GHOST? DEATH DIDN'T SUIT YOU?
WELL... I NEVER WANTED TO BE DEAD, SURFER. FRANKLY, I ONLY DIED OUT OF PEER PRESSURE.
AND THERE ARE OPPORTUNITIES IN THE AFTERWORLDS...IF YOU MEET THE RIGHT PEOPLE.
BUSINESS OPPORTUNITIES.

WHERE ARE YOU TAKING THE TRAIN, NEBULON?
THE SOL SYSTEM.
THE GRAVITATIONAL FORCES ALONE WILL REDUCE EARTH TO DUST.
OVER SEVEN BILLION SOULS--SNUFFED OUT IN AN INSTANT. BECAUSE I WILLED IT...
I THINK NOT.
MY MASTER HAS HIS OWN PLANS FOR THE TRAIN--AS DO I. YOU HAVE NO PLACE IN THEM.
AND AGAINST THE POWER COSMIC, DIMINISHED THOUGH IT IS HERE, YOU HAVE NO--
ACCKK!
NO HOPE? NO--NOT WITHOUT POWERFUL MYSTIC FORCES ON MY SIDE.
GUESS WHAT, NORRIN RADD?
IT'S TRUE. IN DEATH, NEBULON HAS ACQUIRED POWERS FAR GREATER THAN HE HAD IN LIFE.
THE TRAIN ROLLS ON...AND HOPE IS LOST.
FORTUNATEL
I HAVE A PLA

MY NAME IS STEPHEN STRANGE--BUT NOT THIS WORLD'S STRANGE. NOT ANYMORE.
NOW I'M HERE--TO CREATE A TIMELINE WHERE MY FUTURE DOESN'T HAPPEN.
I AM A DEAD MAN FROM A DOOMED FUTURE--ONE WHERE NEBULON SUCCEEDED.
UH-HUH. SO BLOW UP THE TRAIN.
PROBLEM SOLVED.
THIS IS THE HULK. A DARK HULK, INFECTED BY SOMETHING DARKER YET. I CAME TO KNOW HIM WELL IN MY OWN TIME.
FOR WHAT I HAVE PLANNED, HE'S EXACTLY WHAT I NEED.
"WHERE I'M FROM, HULK, THEY DID JUST THAT.
"THE TERRIBLE DECISION WAS MADE, AND WORLDS WERE BURNED IN FIRE...THEIR ENERGY CONSUMED...
"...BUT NOT ALL OF IT. NOT SO MANY PLANETS AT ONCE.
"THE TRAIN WAS STOPPED. THE RADIATION FROM THE EXPLOSION WASN'T. IT SPREAD LIKE A WAVE, KILLING DOZENS OF LIVING WORLDS IN ITS PATH..."

...INCLUDING EARTH.
AND THAT WAS ONLY THE START. TRUST ME WHEN I SAY THINGS GOT A LOT WORSE.
HNH. I'LL STILL SURVIVE...
TRUE. BUT YOU WON'T ENJOY IT MUCH.
I'LL MAKE THIS SIMPLE, HULK. I DESTROYED WHAT WAS LEFT OF MY EARTH TO RETURN HERE--BUT THE SPELL COST MY LIFE, TOO.
MY ASTRAL FORM HAS LESS THAN AN HOUR BEFORE IT DISSIPATES--AND I DIE THE TRUE DEATH. AND MY MAGIC IS DISSIPATING, TOO.
I CAN'T WASTE WHAT I HAVE LEFT ON COMBAT. I NEED SOMEONE TO HELP ME...
...SMASH, AS IT WERE.
EVERYBODY NEEDS SOMETHING.
ME AND BANNER HAVE OUR OWN PROBLEMS RIGHT NOW--
I KNOW. SOMETHING'S INFECTED YOU--AN ENTITY FROM FAR BELOW OUR REALITY.
I MAY KNOW SOMEONE WHO CAN HELP WITH THAT--LATER.
WHERE WE'RE GOING NOW...DARKNESS IS A WEAPON.
I HAVE ENOUGH ENERGY FOR TRANSPORTATION TO WHERE WE NEED TO GO.
BUT SHAPING THE NECESSARY PORTAL TAKES TIME...

...AND IN HELL, TIME IS ALWAYS RUNNING OUT.
NO MATTER WHICH HELL. EVERY SENTIENT SPECIES HAS AN AFTERLIFE--SOME HAVE MANY. HELLS ARE COMMON.
...AND THEY ALL TRADE.
OUR INVESTMENT PERFORMS ADMIRABLY, BORSS. HE USES THE POWER WE GAVE HIM WELL...
LET'S HOPE, MOG'RYS. IF EARTH ISN'T DESTROYED, IT'LL END BADLY FOR US.
WE BORROWED TWO BILLION HUMAN SOULS FROM MEPHISTO AND SOLD THEM TO THE SPIRIT-FLAYERS OF CARCOSA--SO WE'RE RICH NOW--
VERY RICH.
--BUT EVENTUALLY, MEPHISTO WILL WANT THOSE SOULS BACK.
IF EARTH DIES--SEVEN BILLION OF THAT SOUL TYPE HITTING THE MARKETS AT ONCE--HUMAN SOUL PRICES CRASH.
WE CAN BUY FRESH HUMAN SOULS CHEAP, PAY MEPHISTO BACK WITH THOSE... AND PROFIT.
YES, YES. I KNOW HOW TO SHORT A SOUL, BROTHER.

BUT THEY ARE ALL *LINKED*...
BUT IF EARTH *DOESN'T* DIE? W-WE'LL...OWE OUR *OWN* SOULS...
...A *BILLION TIMES OVER*...
YOU'RE *WORRYING* TOO MUCH, BORSS. NEBULON *WILL* DELIVER.
HE'S MANIPULATED LESSER BEINGS FOR HIS OWN SELFISH REASONS *THROUGHOUT* HIS LIFE. HE SHARES OUR *POLITICS.*
HE'S ONE OF *US.*
SO *HE* WILL SIT AT OUR *RIGHT PAW*--AS OUR FELLOW *DEMONS* SQUABBLE AND DEBASE THEMSELVES FOR A *TASTE* OF OUR NEWFOUND WEALTH.
AND THEN... WILL WE EAT THEIR *FACES,* BROTHER?
OH YES.
WE'LL EAT *ALL* THE FACES.

MORE SPEED, CONDUCTOR!
ANOTHER WORLD INTO THE COSMIC FIRE!
N-NO--NO MORE--
NO MORE DEATH--
AREN'T YOU DEAD YET, NORRIN RADD?
WELL, NOT LONG NOW. I'M LEECHING YOUR COSMIC POWER, AND THE TRAIN IS PICKING UP SPEED.
YOU AND THAT MUDBALL THAT KILLED ME WILL SOON BE VERY DEAD.
NOBODY'S COMING TO SAVE YOU...
AN ENTRANCE LINE IF EVER I HEARD ONE.
BUT NOT MINE.

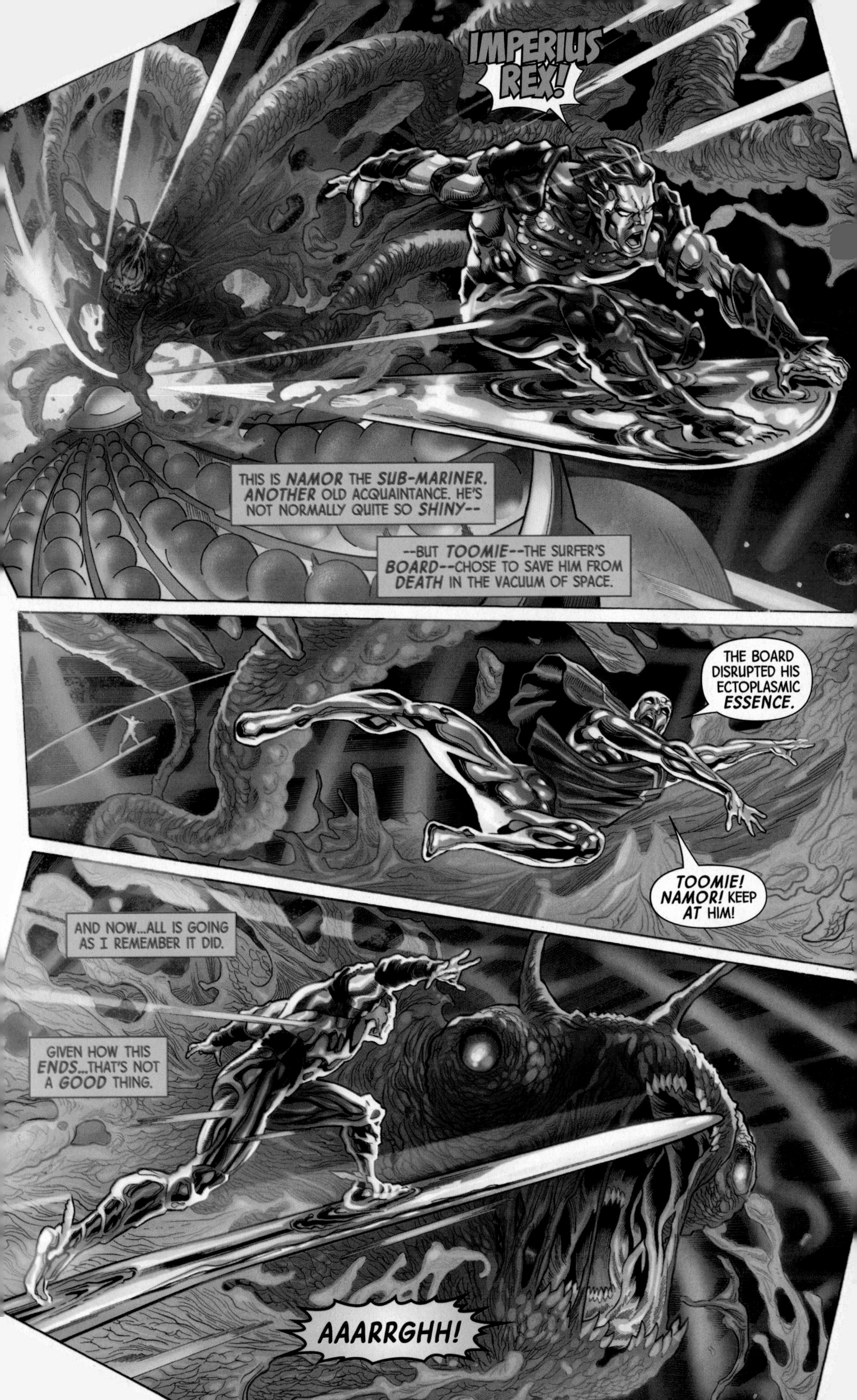
IMPERIUS REX!
THIS IS NAMOR THE SUB-MARINER. ANOTHER OLD ACQUAINTANCE. HE'S NOT NORMALLY QUITE SO SHINY--
--BUT TOOMIE--THE SURFER'S BOARD--CHOSE TO SAVE HIM FROM DEATH IN THE VACUUM OF SPACE.
THE BOARD DISRUPTED HIS ECTOPLASMIC ESSENCE.
TOOMIE! NAMOR! KEEP AT HIM!
AND NOW...ALL IS GOING AS I REMEMBER IT DID.
GIVEN HOW THIS ENDS...THAT'S NOT A GOOD THING.
AAARRGHH!

SO...
NO!
I-IF THESE ACTIVISTS DEFEAT NEBULON--
EVEN IF THEY DO--IT'S TOO LATE.
THE CONDUCTOR'S FAMILIARS ARE DEAD. THEY CAN'T CHANGE THE TRAIN'S COURSE--THEY CAN ONLY DESTROY IT. WHICH KILLS THE EARTH ANYWAY.
RELAX, MY BROTHER. THERE'S NOTHING THAT CAN GO...
...WRONG...
UH-OH.
YOU JINXED IT.
...LET'S ALTER THE NARRATIVE.

HOW DARE YOU, SIR! THIS IS A PLACE OF BUSINESS!
RROOWRR!
YEAH. THAT WAS A MISTAKE.
SEE...MY BUSINESS IS HURTING PEOPLE.
AND IT'S HUNGRY WORK.
AAAHH!
NO! STOP!
STOP!
AAEEIIIGH!
I--I NEVER THOUGHT ANYONE WOULD EAT OUR FACES...

MM-MMM. TASTES LIKE CHICKEN.
WHO'S NEXT?
M-MUH-- MUH--
MUMSY!
WHAT THE HELL...?
THEY'RE ONLY MINOR DEMONS-- THEIR PHYSICAL BODIES ARE NO MATCH FOR YOU IN YOUR CURRENT FORM. BUT PHYSICAL BODIES ARE A LUXURY THEY CAN GIVE UP.
AFTER ALL, THEY CAN ALWAYS BUY NEW ONES...
...AND THEIR ESSENCE CAN BE PUT TO BETTER USE ELSEWHERE.

"THE REAL FIGHT IS JUST BEGINNING," I TELL HIM.
I FEEL... POWER...
SO MUCH POWER!
BY SEDNA'S EYES--
IT IS AN UNDERSTATEMENT.
IN AN INSTANT, NAMOR IS FLUNG BACK TO THE DEPTHS OF SPACE--THIS TIME WITHOUT THE PROTECTION OF THE SURFER'S BOARD.
NAMOR!
AND NOW, NORRIN HAS A CHOICE TO MAKE.
JOIN WITH HIS BOARD AGAIN--KEEP NEBULON OCCUPIED, IF NOT DEFEATED--OR USE IT TO RESCUE HIS FRIEND, THUS CONDEMNING MORE WORLDS TO THE TRAIN'S FURNACE.
AND EITHER WAY, EARTH IS LOST. AN IMPOSSIBLE DECISION...

...EVEN IF WE LET HIM MAKE IT.
C'MERE, SHINY. YOU'RE GOING AFTER HIM.
HULK? IS THAT YOU?
WAIT-- I'LL NEED MY--
--BOOOAAARDD!
DON'T WORRY, RADD--
--I'LL TAKE REAL GOOD CARE OF IT.
AARRGH!
AS TOOMIE'S PSYCHIC SCREAM FILLS MY THIRD EAR, I FEEL MY CONSCIENCE STING--LIKE A PHANTOM PAIN FROM AN ORGAN LONG DEAD.

I WONDER IF NORRIN HEARS IT TOO.
NAMOR!
HULK'S AIM WAS TRUE-- BUT WITHOUT MY BOARD, I CANNOT--
AFTER ALL...
AH. OF COURSE.
SUCH AN ELEGANT SOLUTION...
...THE SURFER...
...AND THE BOARD...
...ARE ONE.
...
THIS IS RIDICULOUS.
YOU THINK SO?
I CONSIDER IT SUBLIME.

STOP IT! STOP HITTING ME!
VIOLENCE ISN'T THE ANSWER!
THAT'S WHAT THEY ALL SAY--
THE HULK IS AN EXCELLENT DISTRACTION. HE'S BOUGHT VALUABLE MOMENTS...
...MOMENTS THE WATER PLANET OF VODAN--RECENTLY VISITED BY NAMOR--WOULD NOT OTHERWISE HAVE.
FOR IT HAS REACHED THE HEAD OF THE QUEUE...
...FOR THE FURNACE.
THE WATER IS WARMING. I--I CAN SEE FLAMES--
WE'LL BE BOILED ALIVE!
PRINCESS--SORRY, QUEEN KATAW--WHAT DO WE DO?
WE MAKE PEACE WITH OUR ANCESTORS.
I WILL SEE YOU SOON, FATHER.
BUT I HAVE PLANNED THIS FOR THOUSANDS OF YEARS. I FORESAW EVERY MOMENT--EACH EVENT IN THE CHAIN.
NEBULON CONCENTRATES ON THE HULK...AND GIVES ME MY MOMENT...

...TO SLIDE MY ASTRAL FORM INTO THE MACRO-MIND OF THE CONDUCTOR.
I DO NOT HAVE NEBULON'S LEVEL OF POWER. I CANNOT CONTROL HIM.
BUT IF I EXERT ALL MY WILL-- ALL MY DWINDLING STRENGTH--
--I CAN, PERHAPS-- INDUCE--
--A SPASM.
THE CONDUCTOR'S WAND JERKS.
AND A PLANET OF SOULS IN MY CARE IS HURLED FROM THE FIRE INTO THE DEPTHS...TO FACE A FREEZING DOOM, FAR FROM ANY SUN...

...FAR FROM ANYONE WHO MIGHT HELP THEM.
THAT PLANET-- THAT IS VODAN, SURFER. A WORLD PEOPLED BY ATLANTEANS.
MY PEOPLE, WHETHER THEY LIKE IT OR NOT. AND I WON'T LET THEM DIE...
NO. NOR I.
PERHAPS... USING THE POWER COSMIC...
...THERE ARE ORPHAN SUNS, WITHOUT WORLDS. IF I COULD CREATE A WORMHOLE TO ONE SUCH STAR...
...THERE IS A CHANCE. BUT THE ENERGIES IT WOULD TAKE...
I AM SEPARATED FROM MY BOARD. DRAINED FROM THE BATTLE WITH NEBULON. I AM... TOO WEAK.
GALACTUS IS THE SOURCE OF THE POWER COSMIC--BUT HE IS FAR FROM HERE, AT THE BACK OF THE TRAIN. I DOUBT HE WOULD EVEN HEAR US--
WE MAY NOT NEED HIM TO.
IF GALACTUS IS THE SOURCE OF YOUR POWER...IF HE GENERATES IT FROM THE ENERGY HE TAKES IN...
SURFER-- CAN YOU FOCUS THOSE PLANET-FINDING SENSES OF YOURS ON A SINGLE PERSON?
IT IS EASIER IF I KNOW THEM, BUT... YES. YOU HAVE A PLAN?
OF SORTS.

"I'M GOING TO CUT OUT THE MIDDLEMAN."
IT-- IT GROWS COLDER, MY LADY, AND OUR TECHNOLOGIES FAIL US--WE WILL ALL FREEZE IN THE VOID OF SPACE--
THEN FREEZE WITH DIGNITY, CURSE YOU!
ALL OF YOU! WE WILL FIGHT THIS FATE TO THE LAST, I SWEAR! USING ALL OUR POWER--BUT NONE OF OUR FEAR!
IF THIS WHOLE WORLD TURNS TO ICE--LET THE ICE PRESERVE NOT PANIC, BUT PRIDE AND NOBILITY!
LET US GO TO OUR GRAVES AS VODANI--
--AS THE TRUE ATLANTEANS!
TRUE ATLANTEANS?
WE ARE ALL THE TRUE ATLANTEANS, QUEEN KATAW.
YOU!
A LESSON YOUR FATHER SHOULD HAVE LEARNED SOONER.
YOU DARE TO SPEAK OF HIM? YOU CHOKED HIM TO DEATH IN FRONT OF ME!
TO EVEN RETURN HERE-- YOU ARE REGICIDE, NAMOR! SLAYER OF KINGS!
YOU KILLED HER FATHER?
THREATS TO MY PERSON ARE ONE THING.
THREATS TO MY PEOPLE...ARE ANOTHER.
SO I ASK NO FORGIVENESS, FOR IT WOULD CHEAPEN US BOTH. KILL ME IF YOU WISH.
BUT I OFFER RESPECT BETWEEN MONARCHS...AND A WAY TO SAVE YOUR WORLD.

KATAW, YOU HAVE THE POWER TO ABSORB AND REDIRECT ELECTRICITY. WHICH, I ASSUME, INCLUDES BIO-ELECTRICITY.
THE ENERGY OF LIFE.
DO YOU RECOGNIZE MY COLLEAGUE?
THE SILVER MAN.
THE HERALD.
I SEE YOU DO.
HIS IS THE POWER COSMIC. HE CAN USE IT TO SAVE THIS WORLD...BUT HIS FLAME BURNS LOW.
NAMOR...?
HE NEEDS NOURISHMENT-- A MEAL FIT FOR HIS MASTER. AND IF WE HAVE LEARNED ANYTHING FROM GALACTUS...
...IT IS THAT LIFE FORCE RECHARGES HIS POWER.
NO...
SO-- TAKE SOME OF MINE.
I OFFER IT GLADLY...AS THE KING...
...FOR MY PEOPLE.

I CANNOT ACCEPT YOUR DEATH, NAMOR. ANY DEATH.
BUT IF... IF YOU ARE WILLING TO SACRIFICE...SOME LIFE FORCE FOR YOUR PEOPLE...
YOU AS WELL?
HIS PEOPLE. AGAIN AND AGAIN, HIS PEOPLE. A CULTURE HE HAS NEVER KNOWN, COULD NEVER UNDERSTAND--
--BUT IN HE PADDLES, AND SUDDENLY WE'RE HIS PEOPLE. AND WHAT DOES HE OFFER HIS PEOPLE?
PETULANCE, ARROGANCE, VIOLENCE...EMPTY, POSTURING OBEISANCE...
...INSIGNIFICANCE.
AND YOU.
WHO ARE YOU TO BE THE JUDGE OF WORLDS? PROTECTED FROM LIFE IN YOUR SILVER SHELL?
YOU WILL NOT ACCEPT DEATH?
YOU THINK YOU GET TO CHOOSE?
LOOK WELL, NAMOR. THIS IS WHY YOU WILL NEVER RULE US.
WHEN WE GO TO MEET OUR DEATHS--VODANI DO NOT KNEEL!
NO!

NO! PLEASE, NO!
NOT THIS--
NOT THIS!
HIS SCREAM TEARS A HOLE IN THE SKIN OF SPACE.
A DOORWAY TO A LONELY SUN. TO WARMTH AND GRAVITY. TO LIFE.
EVEN IN THE DEPTH OF HIS HORROR, THE SURFER'S GRASP OF SPATIAL MECHANICS IS EXCELLENT.
POOR NORRIN RADD.
HE IS ONE OF THE MOST POWERFUL BEINGS IN THE UNIVERSE...
ALL HAIL! NOW AND FOREVER--
--ALL HAIL QUEEN KATAW!
...BUT SOME THINGS CAN NEVER BE OVERCOME.

SOME PART OF BRUCE BANNER WILL ALWAYS BE A CREATURE OF RAGE.
NEBULON WILL ALWAYS BE A DIM-WITTED PUPPET FOR ANY HALF-BAKED SCHEME GOING-- INCLUDING HIS OWN.
A COSMIC CON ARTIST FOREVER DOOMED TO BELIEVE HIS OWN HYPE.
AND ME? STEPHEN STRANGE, WHO HAS CHANGED SO VERY MUCH? WHO LOST HIS FRIENDS, HIS HOME, HIS LIFE, EVEN HIS POSITION AS THE "TRUE" STEPHEN STRANGE?
I'M A MAGICIAN BECAUSE I CHANGED--BECAUSE I TURNED AWAY FROM THE MATERIAL WORLD. BUT STILL...
...PART OF ME WILL ALWAYS REMEMBER A LITTLE HIGH SCHOOL SCIENCE.
SPECIFICALLY, NEWTON'S THIRD LAW.
IT'S OVER, NEBULON. YOU'VE LOST.
YOU JUST DON'T KNOW IT YET.
TOO LATE FOR BRAVADO, STRANGE.
WHILE YOUR PET MONSTER FAILED TO STOP ME, THE TRAIN HAS ROLLED ON--AND IN SECONDS, IT WILL REDUCE YOUR PATHETIC SOLAR SYSTEM TO...
TO...

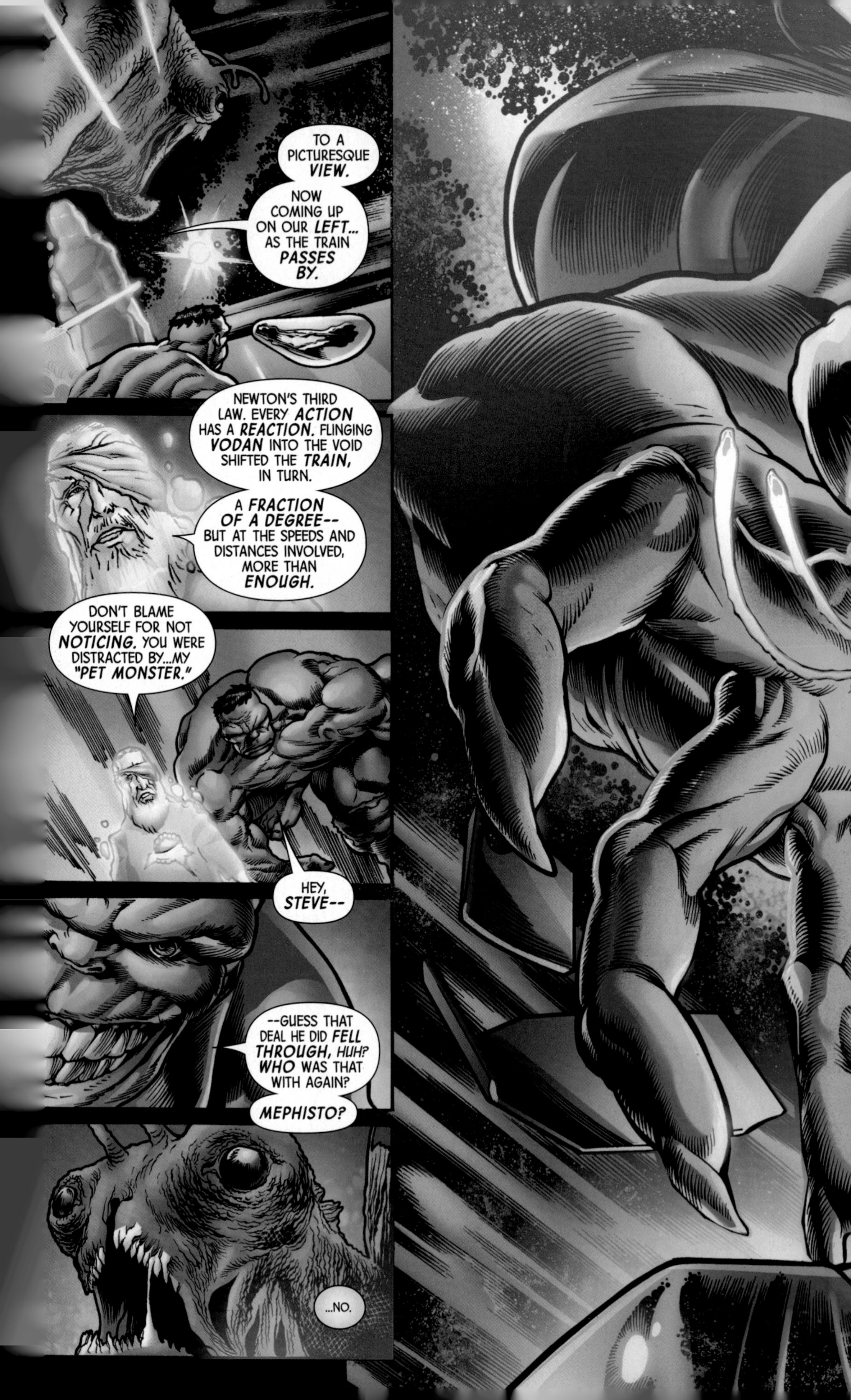
TO A PICTURESQUE VIEW.
NOW COMING UP ON OUR LEFT... AS THE TRAIN PASSES BY.
NEWTON'S THIRD LAW. EVERY ACTION HAS A REACTION. FLINGING VODAN INTO THE VOID SHIFTED THE TRAIN, IN TURN.
A FRACTION OF A DEGREE-- BUT AT THE SPEEDS AND DISTANCES INVOLVED, MORE THAN ENOUGH.
DON'T BLAME YOURSELF FOR NOT NOTICING. YOU WERE DISTRACTED BY...MY "PET MONSTER."
HEY, STEVE--
--GUESS THAT DEAL HE DID FELL THROUGH, HUH? WHO WAS THAT WITH AGAIN?
MEPHISTO?
...NO.

OH YES.
STEPHEN. HULK.
ALWAYS A PLEASURE...
NO! NO! NOOOO!
BE ABOUT YOUR BUSINESS QUICKLY, DARK ONE.
WE HAVE BUSINESS OF OUR OWN...
STEVE?
MY POWER IS GONE. I AM ALMOST GONE. AND THE HULK MUST BE RETURNED HOME-- CURED OF HIS SPIRITUAL INFECTION, IF POSSIBLE--
OH, IT'S NOT.
THE DEVIL IN HIM IS FAR STRONGER THAN I AM. BUT I CAN RETURN HIM TO EARTH...
...FOR A SMALL CONSIDERATION.
"I'M SURPRISED THEY DIDN'T HOLD YOU TO ACCOUNT, NAMOR..."

FOR KILLING ONE MONARCH AND ASSISTING IN THE DEATH OF ANOTHER?
YOU SAID YOURSELF--YOU WON'T LET THEM KILL ME. WHICH LEAVES EXILE...
...AND DISGRACE.
AH-- TOOMIE HAS RETURNED.
AND EARTH IS OUT OF DANGER, IT SEEMS.
DOCTOR STRANGE AND THE HULK FINISHED WHAT WE BEGAN...
THOSE TWO. OF COURSE.
ANOTHER EXCITING NON-TEAM-UP FOR THE DEFENDERS. LET'S ALL HAVE SHAWARMA SOMETIME.
IF YOU'LL EXCUSE ME, I HAVE A MYSTERIOUS MAGIC TUNNEL TO CATCH...
NAMOR.
WAIT.
DID YOU KNOW?
WHEN YOU BROUGHT ME HERE...DID YOU KNOW WHAT WOULD HAPPEN?
...
I WANTED TO MAKE THE SACRIFICE.
TO SAVE KATAW'S WORLD...
...AND UNDERMINE HER RULE. FROM THERE, I COULD HAVE FORCED AN ALLIANCE--USED THE VODANI TO FURTHER MY ENDS.
BUT SHE WAS RIGHT. I DIDN'T UNDERSTAND THEIR CULTURE.
I WAS ARROGANT, AS EVER. AND... AS EVER...

"...ANOTHER PAID THE COST FOR IT."
I HAVE RETURNED, O GALACTUS.
YOU HAVE. AND I SENSE DEATH ON YOU, HERALD.
A LIFE SPENT TO GIVE YOU THE ENERGY YOU NEEDED...
I...WAS GIVEN NO CHOICE. I PROTESTED, BUT NO ONE HEARD ME.
FOR ALL MY POWER, I WAS TREATED AS...ONLY POWER. AS THE DEUS EX MACHINA IN SOME GREAT DRAMA OF WORLDS.
WITHOUT MY BIDDING. WITHOUT MY CONSENT...
AH.
THEN YOU BEGIN TO UNDERSTAND.
COME, NORRIN. YOU AND I HAVE FAR TO GO TOGETHER YET.
AND THERE IS WORK TO BE DONE.
THE TRAIN ROLLS ON.

AND HOPE IS LOST.
THERE. THE HULK IS HOME AND DRY.
EVERYONE'S WHERE THEY BELONG...
...INCLUDING YOU.
I KNOW YOU THINK YOU'RE TRICKING ME SOMEHOW, DOCTOR.
YOU SEE MY DOMAIN AS SOME SAFE HARBOR FOR YOUR TIME-LOST SOUL. YOU THINK YOU MIGHT ESCAPE...AND LIVE AGAIN...
BUT YOU'VE TRICKED YOURSELF. THERE'S NO ESCAPE.
YOU ARE POWERLESS, DEAD AND DAMNED--NO LONGER EVEN THE TRUE STEPHEN STRANGE. NOBODY WILL BOTHER TO REMEMBER YOU.
NO TEAM IS COMING TO SAVE YOU...
FORTUNATELY...
...I HAVE A PLAN.
END.

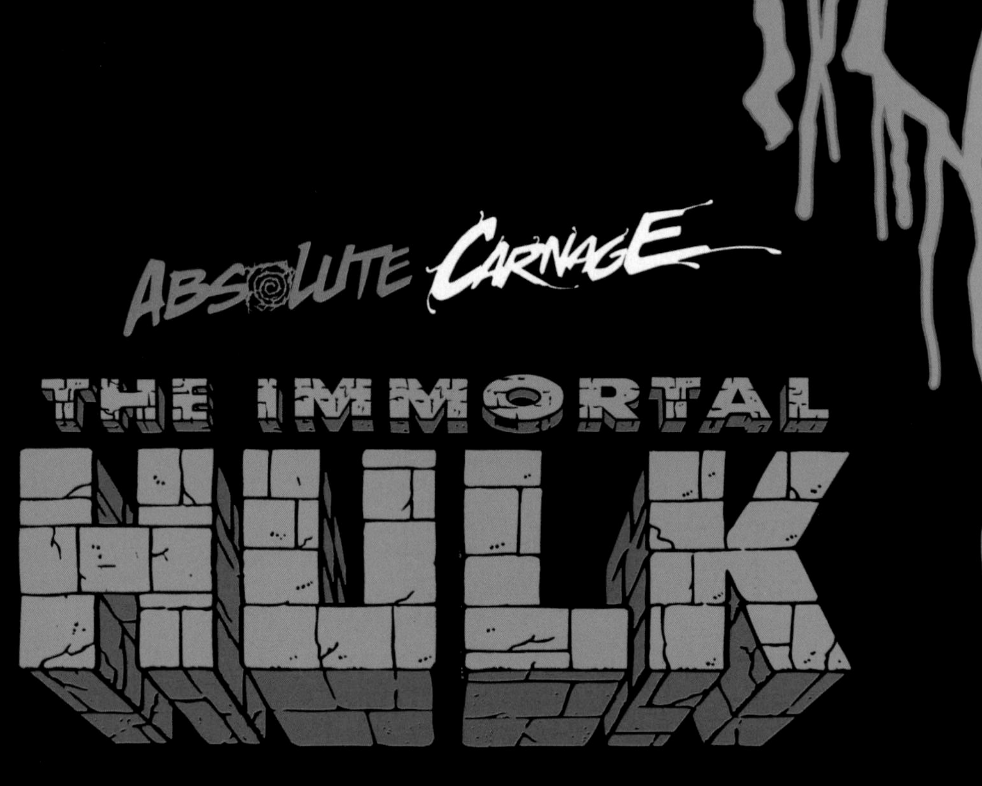

NUCLEAR PHYSICIST BRUCE BANNER, AFTER BEING EXPOSED TO A GAMMA BOMB EXPLOSION, BECAME THE INCREDIBLE, IMMORTAL HULK.

CLETUS KASADY, THE SERIAL KILLER BONDED TO THE CARNAGE SYMBIOTE, IS ON THE HUNT FOR SMALL PIECES OF GENETIC MATERIAL — CALLED "CODICES" — LEFT IN THE SPINE OF ANY BEING WHO HAS BONDED WITH A SYMBIOTE. CARNAGE DOES THIS IN AN ATTEMPT TO FREE HIS GOD, KNULL, AND BRING CHAOS TO EARTH.

BUT THE **HULK** HAS NEVER BEEN BONDED TO A SYMBIOTE...

WARNING: THE EVENTS OF THIS STORY TAKE PLACE *AFTER* **ABSOLUTE CARNAGE #3.** IF YOU HAVEN'T READ IT YET, PROCEED AT YOUR OWN RISK!

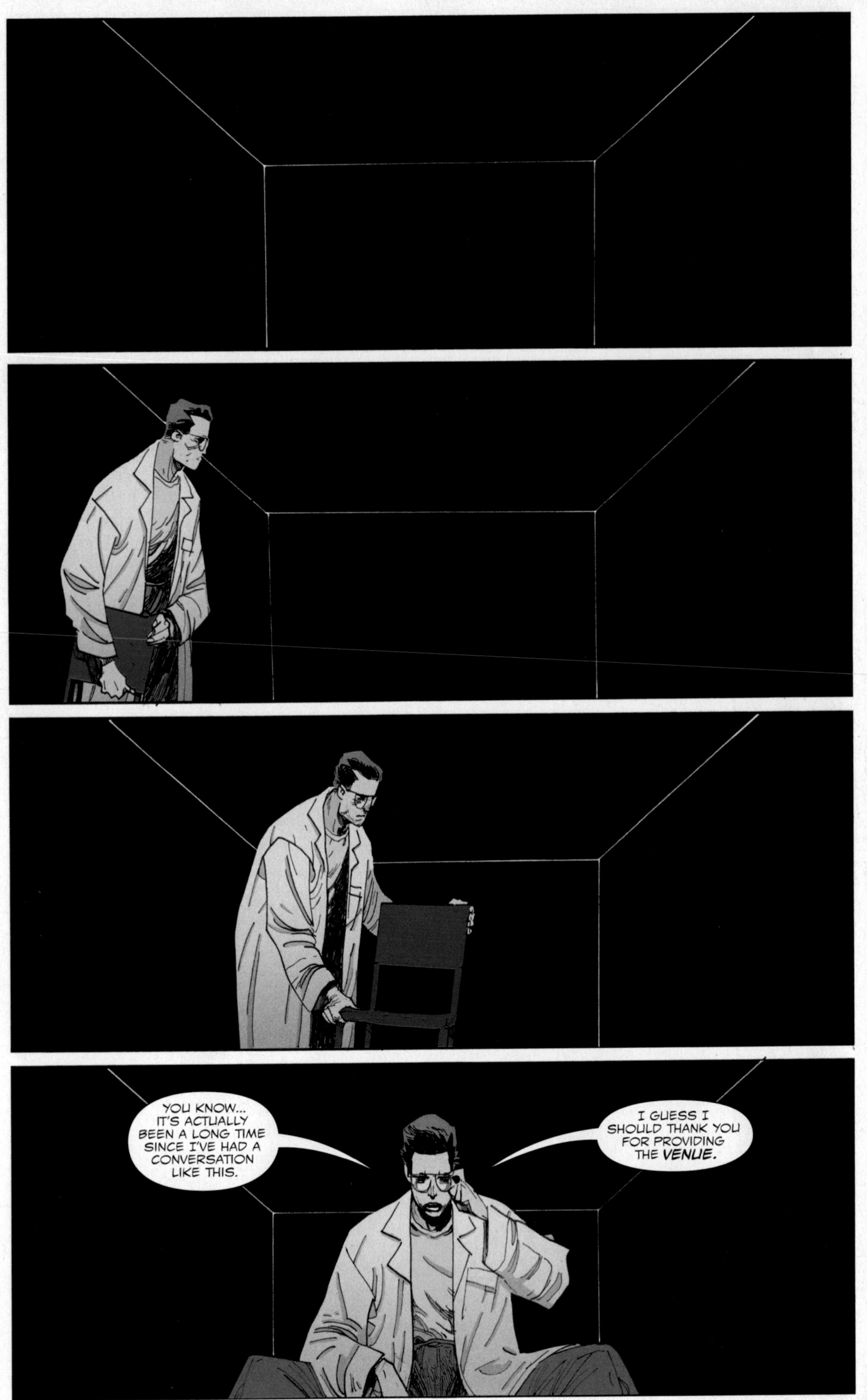
YOU KNOW... IT'S ACTUALLY BEEN A LONG TIME SINCE I'VE HAD A CONVERSATION LIKE THIS.
I GUESS I SHOULD THANK YOU FOR PROVIDING THE *VENUE.*

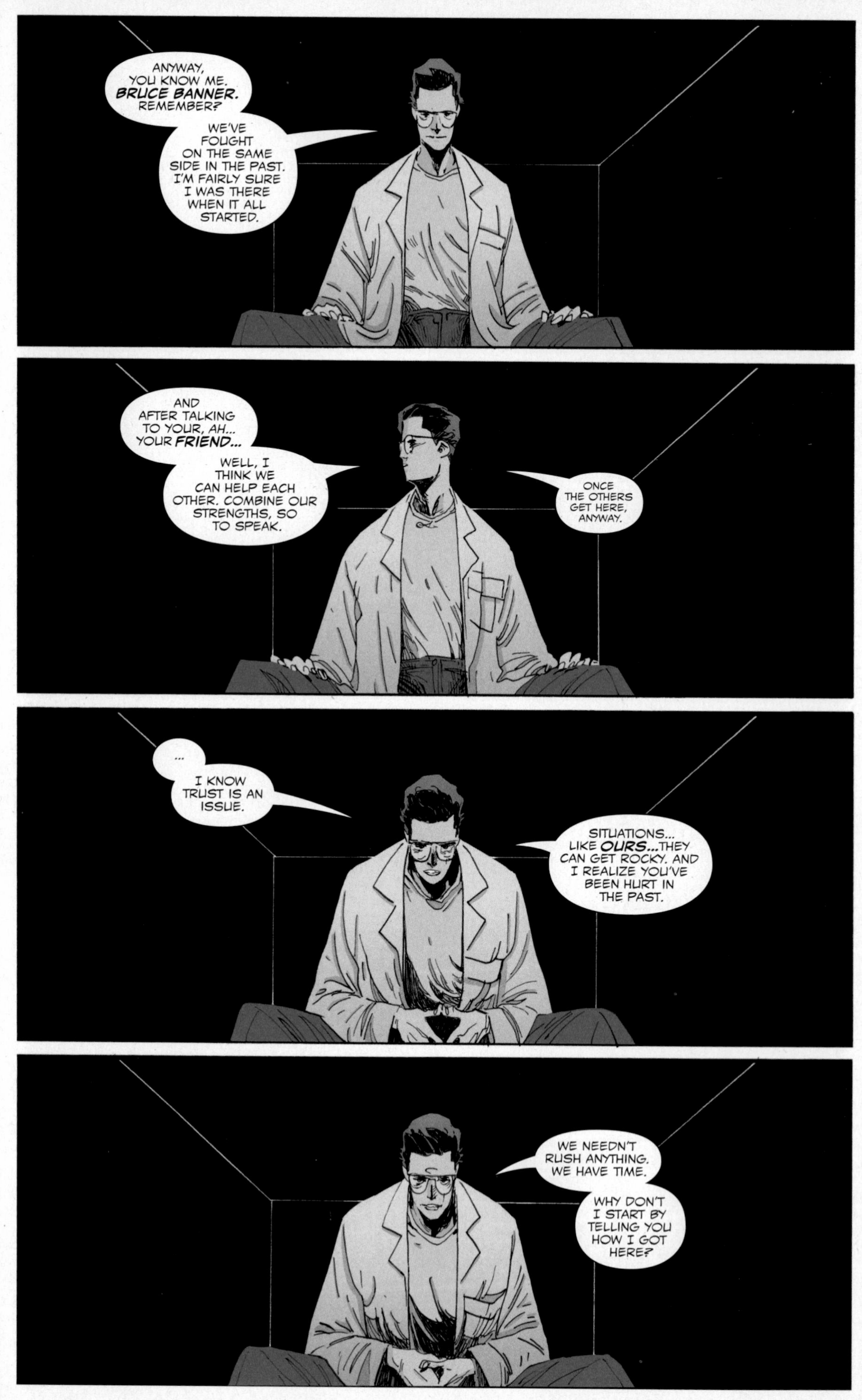
ANYWAY, YOU KNOW ME. **BRUCE BANNER.** REMEMBER?
WE'VE FOUGHT ON THE SAME SIDE IN THE PAST. I'M FAIRLY SURE I WAS THERE WHEN IT ALL STARTED.
AND AFTER TALKING TO YOUR, AH... YOUR **FRIEND...**
WELL, I THINK WE CAN HELP EACH OTHER. COMBINE OUR STRENGTHS, SO TO SPEAK.
ONCE THE OTHERS GET HERE, ANYWAY.
...
I KNOW TRUST IS AN ISSUE.
SITUATIONS... LIKE **OURS...** THEY CAN GET ROCKY. AND I REALIZE YOU'VE BEEN HURT IN THE PAST.
WE NEEDN'T RUSH ANYTHING. WE HAVE TIME.
WHY DON'T I START BY TELLING YOU HOW I GOT HERE?

"BUT **ME...**WELL, WHEN THE TIME COMES FOR ME TO COME BACK OUT...

"...I NEVER KNOW WHAT HAPPENED."

BANNER - ROOM'S PAID FOR. MCGEE NEXT DOOR. DON'T BUG HER. BETTY + JONES IN BATHROOM. DON'T BUG THEM. YOU'RE TOO NEEDY. CLOTHES ARE YOUR SIZE, DON'T MESS'EM UP. MORE IN WARDROBE, INCLUDING PRE-TORN. DEVIL SAYS LAY LOW FOR NOW. I'LL BE BACK IN 2 DAYS TO SWITCH MOTELS UNLESS JONES WAKES UP.

JOE.

BETTY? ARE YOU IN THERE?
KNOCK KNOCK
YES?
I ONLY JUST CAME TO. DID--DID YOU HEAL FROM THE BULLET WOUND? WHAT EXACTLY IS GOING--
--ON?
YES. THIS IS ME.
WE'VE GOT RICK JONES. HE'S IN THE BATHTUB. GETTING BETTER, MAYBE.
JACKIE CAN TELL YOU MORE.
I--I--
SLAM
BETTY?

"I DID SPEAK TO JACKIE McGEE EVENTUALLY. SHE GAVE ME THE FULL STORY-- AS MUCH AS SHE'D SEEN.

"SHADOW BASE STOLE RICK'S CORPSE--THAT I KNEW. WHAT I DIDN'T KNOW WAS THAT THEY'D EXPERIMENTED ON HIM--TURNED HIM INTO AN ***ABOMINATION.***

"THEY SENT HIM AFTER ME. BETTY AND MS. McGEE BECAME INVOLVED. IT GOT... UNPLEASANT.

"EVENTUALLY HULK TORE RICK FREE OF THE ABOMINATION'S SHELL. SINCE THEN, HE'S BEEN...WELL, ***DEAD*** IS THE WRONG WORD FOR PEOPLE LIKE US.

"RECUPERATING.

"ANYWAY. RIGHT THEN THOUGH, I WAS PUTTING OFF TALKING TO HER. SHE'S A ***REPORTER,*** AFTER ALL--SPEAKING RATIONALLY, IT'S HARD TO SEE WHY THE HULKS ***TRUST*** HER SO MUCH.
"ACCORDING TO THE MOTEL STATIONERY, WE WERE IN CALIFORNIA.

BIP
"I FIGURED I COULD GET THE CONTEXT I NEEDED FROM THE ***LOCAL NEWS.***

"I GOT SOMETHING ELSE.
--IN NATIONAL NEWS--A BIZARRE ACT OF DESECRATION AT A MILITARY GRAVESITE.
OR SOMETHING EVEN WORSE?
ONE BODY HAS BEEN CONFIRMED AS MISSING FROM THE SCENE-- A HERO OF OUR COUNTRY, A PROUD SERVANT OF OUR GOVERNMENT. AN AVENGER.
THE BODY OF GENERAL THADDEUS "THUNDERBOLT" ROSS HAS BEEN--
BZ

WE WEREN'T ALLOWED TO FILM IN WEST POINT CEMETERY ITSELF, BUT ROXX NEWS WAS ABLE TO GET THIS AERIAL FOOTAGE.
DOZENS OF GRAVES VANDALIZED IN THE DEAD OF NIGHT. SPREAD ACROSS THE WRECKED HEADSTONES, A SICKLY RED SLIME--POTENTIALLY SOME UNKNOWN BIOLOGICAL WEAPON.
WAS THIS AN ACT OF TERROR? A LIBERAL PROTEST AGAINST OUR MILITARY?
ROXX NEWS
"THE STOLEN CORPSE OF A KNOWN GAMMA MUTATE. JUST AS RICK'S HAD BEEN STOLEN.
"THERE WAS EVEN RED BIO-MATTER AT THE SCENE--RED FOR THE RED HULK. ROSS' MUTATION.
"THERE WAS ONLY ONE CONCLUSION I COULD POSSIBLY COME TO."

THIS WAS CLEARLY ALL ABOUT ME.
EITHER THIS WAS SHADOW BASE AGAIN--
--A VAST AND SECRET ARM OF THE GOVERNMENT ATTEMPTING TO HARNESS GAMMA MUTATION AS A WEAPON--
--OR IT WAS SOMETHING POTENTIALLY WORSE.
YOU SEE, THE THING ABOUT GAMMA PEOPLE--
HEY!
SO THIS IS HAPPENING, HUH?
YOU SEE THIS? WHAT IS THIS?
UM...

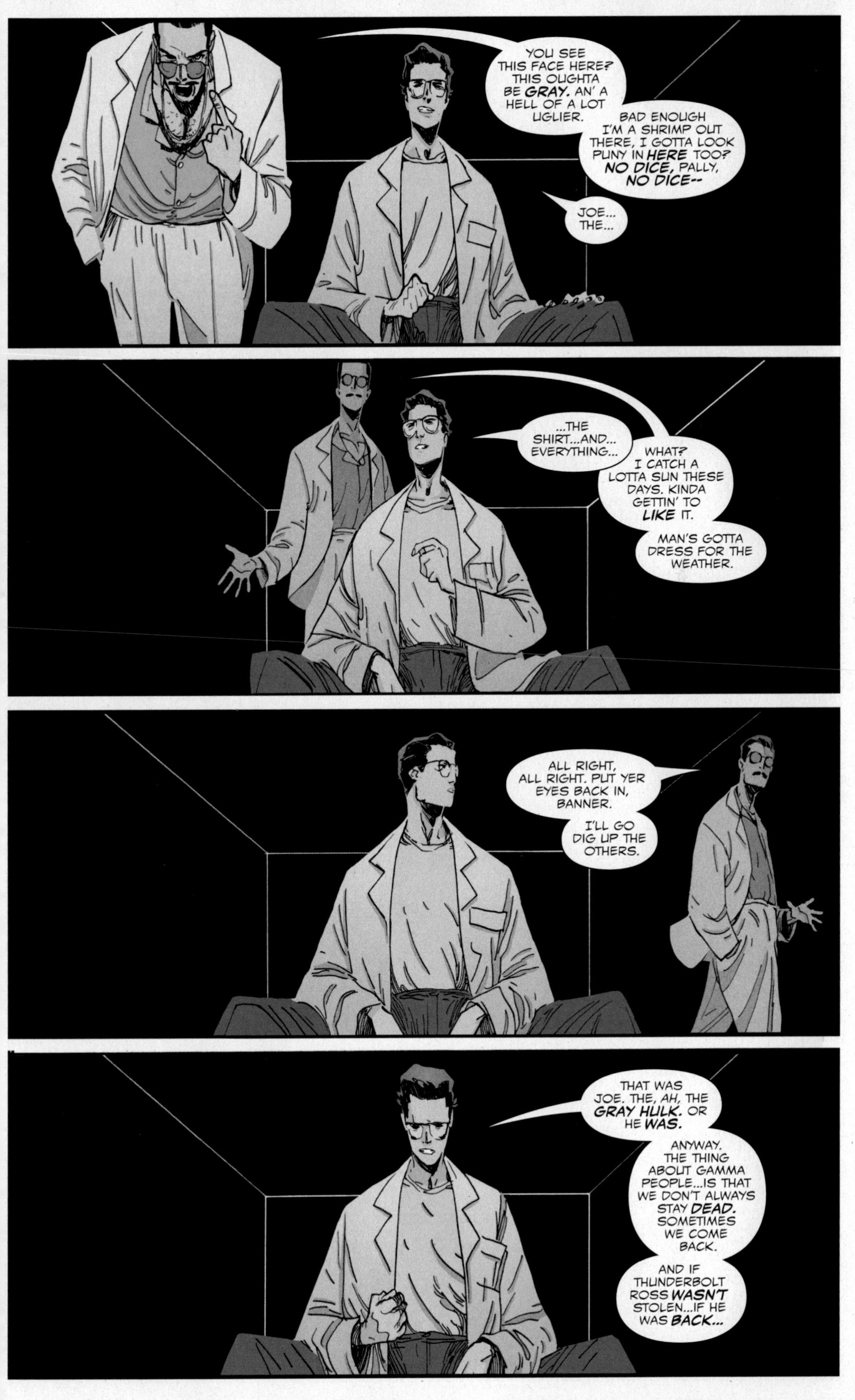
YOU SEE THIS FACE HERE? THIS OUGHTA BE GRAY. AN' A HELL OF A LOT UGLIER.
BAD ENOUGH I'M A SHRIMP OUT THERE, I GOTTA LOOK PUNY IN HERE TOO? NO DICE, PALLY, NO DICE--
JOE... THE...
...THE SHIRT...AND... EVERYTHING...
WHAT? I CATCH A LOTTA SUN THESE DAYS. KINDA GETTIN' TO LIKE IT.
MAN'S GOTTA DRESS FOR THE WEATHER.
ALL RIGHT, ALL RIGHT. PUT YER EYES BACK IN, BANNER.
I'LL GO DIG UP THE OTHERS.
THAT WAS JOE. THE, AH, THE GRAY HULK. OR HE WAS.
ANYWAY. THE THING ABOUT GAMMA PEOPLE...IS THAT WE DON'T ALWAYS STAY DEAD. SOMETIMES WE COME BACK.
AND IF THUNDERBOLT ROSS WASN'T STOLEN...IF HE WAS BACK...

...I THOUGHT YOU SHOULD KNOW.

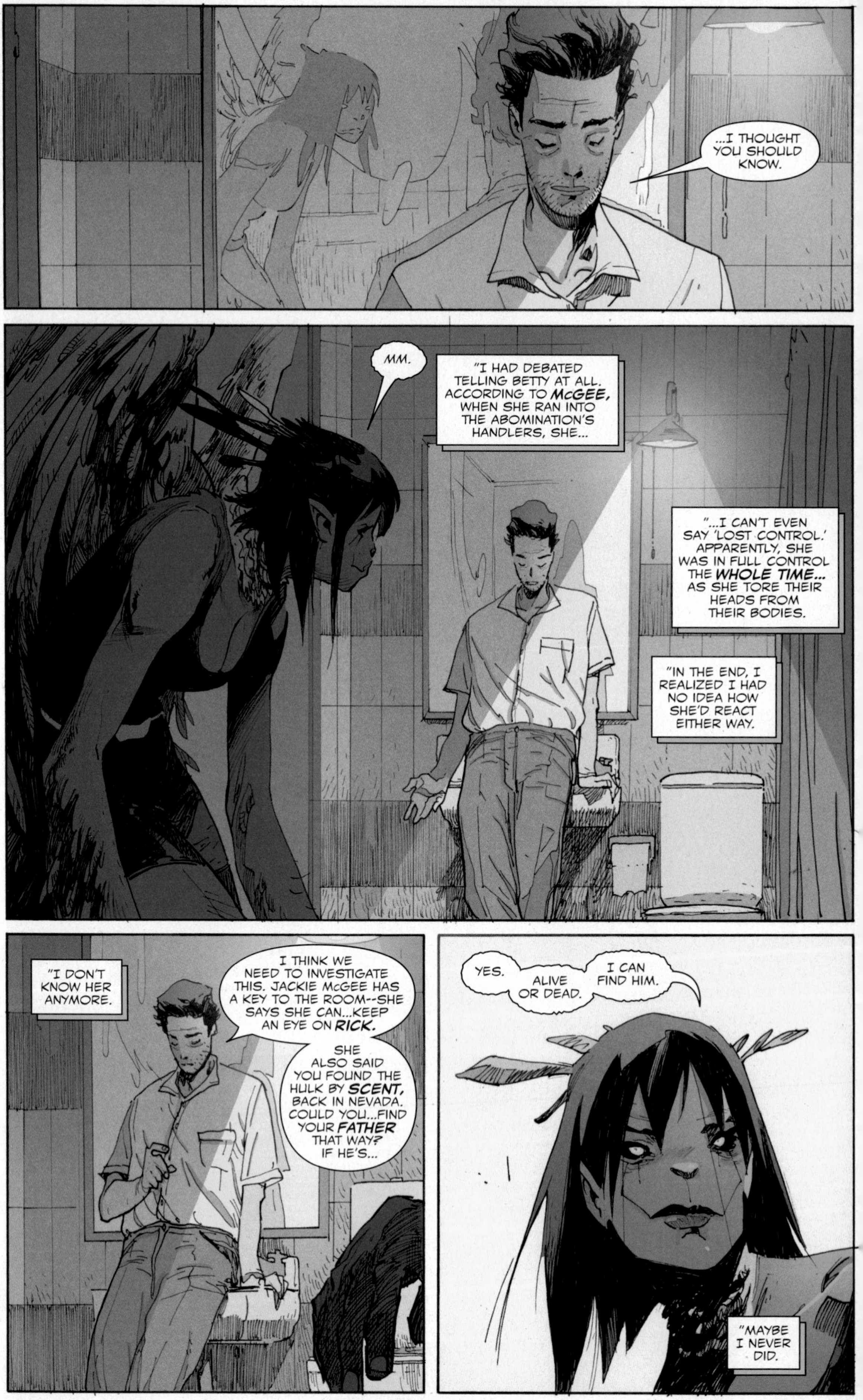

MM.

"I HAD DEBATED TELLING BETTY AT ALL. ACCORDING TO **McGEE,** WHEN SHE RAN INTO THE ABOMINATION'S HANDLERS, SHE...

"...I CAN'T EVEN SAY 'LOST CONTROL.' APPARENTLY, SHE WAS IN FULL CONTROL THE ***WHOLE TIME...*** AS SHE TORE THEIR HEADS FROM THEIR BODIES.

"IN THE END, I REALIZED I HAD NO IDEA HOW SHE'D REACT EITHER WAY.

"I DON'T KNOW HER ANYMORE.
I THINK WE NEED TO INVESTIGATE THIS. JACKIE McGEE HAS A KEY TO THE ROOM--SHE SAYS SHE CAN...KEEP AN EYE ON *RICK.*
SHE ALSO SAID YOU FOUND THE HULK BY *SCENT,* BACK IN NEVADA. COULD YOU...FIND YOUR *FATHER* THAT WAY? IF HE'S...

YES.
ALIVE OR DEAD.
I CAN FIND HIM.
"MAYBE I NEVER DID.

...ALL RIGHT. IN THAT CASE, YOU MIGHT BE THE BEST TRANSPORT TO WEST POINT WE HAVE.
WHAT'S YOUR **AIRSPEED?** HOW QUICKLY CAN YOU GET THERE?
ALONE? TEN HOURS. MAYBE LESS. CARRYING YOU?
LONGER. TOO LONG. WE'D BE SEEN.

...
WHAT IF... YOU...
WHAT IF YOU FOLDED ME UP SMALL?
"SHE SAID NOTHING TO THAT. BUT SHE UNDERSTOOD.
"IT WAS EARLY MORNING. A GOOD TWELVE HOURS BEFORE THE SUN SET AND THE HULK ROSE. THE JOURNEY WOULD BE EASIER IF I... WASN'T THERE.

"SHE TOOK MY FACE IN HER HANDS, ALMOST GENTLY. I HOPED SHE WOULDN'T MAKE A MESS.

THERE WASN'T ANY PAIN.

"I NEVER REMEMBER WHAT HAPPENS WHEN I'M DEAD.

"MAYBE I SHOULD.

MAYBE IT'S IMPORTANT.

OH, **BRUCE.**

SHE JUST KEEPS **KILLING** YOU, DOESN'T SHE?

AND USUALLY I DON'T REMEMBER WHAT THE HULK DOES EITHER. WHILE I'M DEAD OR...AWAY. I TOLD YOU THAT, DIDN'T I?

BUT THIS TIME...

"THIS TIME, HE LET ME REMEMBER.
HNNH!

"THE CHANGE PROBABLY HURT MUCH MORE THAN USUAL. I WAS FOLDED UP SMALL, AFTER ALL. AND THE HULK IS VERY BIG.
"IT WOULD HAVE BEEN LIKE AN AIRBAG INFLATING.
OW.
DAMMIT, BETTY...

"BETTY WAS ALREADY GONE.
"OUR BEST GUESS IS THAT SHE FLEW US TO WEST POINT, GOT HER FATHER'S SCENT FROM HIS GRAVE--
"--AND THEN TRACKED HIM TO WHERE HE WAS NOW.

ROSS...?
"I DON'T KNOW WHY SHE DIDN'T STAY. MAYBE SHE WAS SATISFIED WITH THE ANSWER. MAYBE SHE NEEDED TO BE ALONE.
"MAYBE SHE JUST DIDN'T CARE ABOUT WHAT SHE'D FOUND...

"...BUT I FIND THAT HARD TO BELIEVE."

ANYWAY. FOR WHATEVER REASON, BETTY LEFT US TO DEAL WITH THAT--

BETTY WAS ***HERE?***

HEY, BIG GUY.

BETTY... BETTY IS ***FRIEND.*** OR...***WAS*** FRIEND...

HULK DOES NOT KNOW ANY-MORE.

NO. NO, NEITHER DO I.

HULK ***NEVER*** SEES FRIENDS. HULK ONLY COMES OUT TO ***HURT...*** AND TO ***HURT...***

HULK... HULK ***ALWAYS*** HURTS. ALL THE TIME ALWAYS AND ***ALWAYS.***

WELL... PEOPLE HAVE BEEN ASKING THAT QUESTION SINCE THE DAWN OF TIME, HULK--
BAH!
STUPID BANNER! STUPID BANNER KNOWS NOTHING!
STUPID BANNER TURNED BETTY INTO NOT-FRIEND! STUPID, PUNY BANNER!
I--I DON'T THINK I CAN BE BLAMED FOR--
STUPID BANNER!
...
THE MASS GRAVE WAS IN THE GROUNDS OF AN ABANDONED MENTAL HOSPITAL IN NEW JERSEY.
IT WAS AWAY FROM THE PUBLIC BUT FAR FROM HIDDEN. A LOT OF PEOPLE DO HIKE OUT TO SEE THESE OLD BUILDINGS.
SOMEONE WOULD HAVE FOUND IT. EVENTUALLY.
BUT WE DIDN'T HAVE THAT KIND OF TIME TO GET THE ANSWERS WE NEEDED.
SO THE HULK DID SOMETHING HE'D NEVER DONE BEFORE.

"HE CALLED THE NEWS."
OUR TOP STORY TONIGHT-- AN ANONYMOUS TIP-OFF REVEALS A HORRIFIC SECRET LURKING IN NORTHERN NEW JERSEY.
VIEWERS ARE ADVISED THAT THE IMAGES CONTAINED IN THIS REPORT ARE EXTREMELY GRAPHIC IN NATURE--
SWAT

"EXTREMELY GRAPHIC." YEAH, I'LL SAY. CAN YOU BELIEVE THIS CRAP?
STOLEN CORPSES WITH THEIR SPINES TORN OUT?
CELEBRITY CORPSES TOO.
POLI

SOME BIG-SHOT MILITARY GUYS ALREADY TOOK THUNDERBOLT ROSS OFF OUR HANDS...
GOOD. GREAT. I HOPE THEY TAKE THIS WHOLE MESS OFF OUR HANDS.
I MISS WHEN WE COULD BUMP CRAP LIKE THIS UP THE CHAIN TO S.H.I.E.L.D. OR WHOEVER, Y'KNOW?

I MEAN, WHERE ARE WE MEANT TO EVEN START WITH THIS?
...DIDN'T YOU SAY THERE WAS A MOBSTER'S KID IN THERE?
YEAH, I PULLED HIS JACKET. GOT IT HERE IF YOU WANNA SEE.
ANGELO FORTUNATO, SON OF DON FORTUNATO.

I REMEMBER THE DON. DON'T REMEMBER THE KID--WAS HE EVEN IN THE FAMILY BUSINESS?
ACCORDING TO HIS FILE, IT'S WHAT GOT HIM KILLED.
HE WAS TRYIN' TO MAKE IT AS A SUPER VILLAIN TO IMPRESS HIS OLD MAN. DIDN'T WORK OUT.
TALE AS OLD AS TIME, SONG AS OLD AS RHYME. DID HE GET A COOL COSTUME OUT OF IT, AT LEAST?
OH YEAH. HE GOT A COOL COSTUME, ALL RIGHT.
SAYS HERE FOR ABOUT FIVE MINUTES...
...ANGELO FORTUNATO WAS VENOM.
"PEOPLE DON'T BELIEVE THIS.
"I WOULDN'T BELIEVE IT WITHOUT THE EVIDENCE.
"BUT THE HULK IS ACTUALLY VERY GOOD AT NOT BEING NOTICED.

"HE'S ALSO VERY GOOD AT BEING NOTICED.
OKAY. HEROES, HEROES, HEROES. HEROES WHO WERE VENOMS. WHO'S ON THE LIST?
I THINK CAP? SHOULD BRING HIM IN ON GENERAL PRINCIPLE. UM... WOLVERINE...HAWKEYE... MAYBE BEN GRIMM...
...CAN OF CHICKPEAS... NO, WAIT, THAT'S THE GROCERY LIST...
UGH. SUN'S JUST ABOUT TO COME UP.
I'M RUNNING OUT OF--
--TIME--
OBOY.
"HULK JUST WANTED SPIDER-MAN'S ATTENTION.

"HE KNEW THAT WOULDN'T **HURT** HIM...

"...AND HE WOULDN'T LET IT HURT ANYONE **ELSE.**

THWIP THWIP
THWIP

"OR I **ASSUME** THAT WAS THE THINKING."

OH MY GOODNESS--

I KNOW, RIGHT?

LISTEN, DO ME A FAVOR AND CALL **DAMAGE CONTROL,** HUH? THIS WEBBING MELTS IN AN HOUR--

--AND I GOTTA GO FIGHT **CARNAGE** BEFORE HE--

OH.
HELLO, SPIDER-MAN.
WELL, **THAT** I WAS **NOT** EXPECTING.

YORKER
I CAN'T BELIEVE YOU HAVE CACHES OF **SPARE CLOTHES** HIDDEN ALL OVER THE CITY.
I CAN'T BELIEVE YOU **DON'T.**

WELL, FOR ALL I KNOW, I **DO.** I'M PRETTY SURE I'VE LOST A DAY OR TWO SINCE WE FOUND THAT MASS GRAVE.
THAT MEANS HULK PUT **JOE FIXIT** IN CHARGE TO KEEP US SAFE AND HIDDEN DURING **DAYLIGHT.**
BUT, OF COURSE, JOE DOESN'T LIKE **YOU** AT ALL...

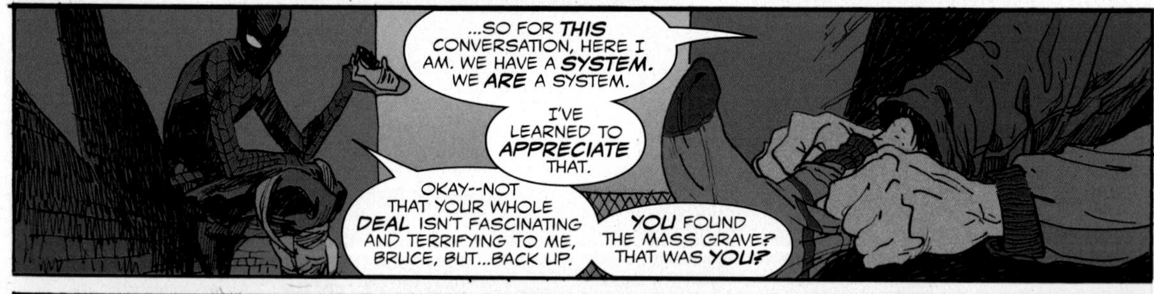

...SO FOR **THIS** CONVERSATION, HERE I AM. WE HAVE A **SYSTEM.** WE **ARE** A SYSTEM.
I'VE LEARNED TO **APPRECIATE** THAT.
OKAY--NOT THAT YOUR WHOLE **DEAL** ISN'T FASCINATING AND TERRIFYING TO ME, BRUCE, BUT...BACK UP.
YOU FOUND THE MASS GRAVE? THAT WAS **YOU?**

THUNDERBOLT ROSS' BODY WAS **STOLEN.** FINDING OUT WHO DID IT AND WHY WAS MY TOP PRIORITY.
HE'S A BIOLOGICAL--A **THEOLOGICAL** WMD. A POTENTIAL DOORWAY TO AN EVIL YOU **CANNOT POSSIBLY COMPREHEND.**
SIZE ELEVEN. THAT'LL DO.

I'M **SERIOUS,** SPIDER-MAN--YOU HAVE **NO IDEA** WHAT I'VE BEEN DEALING WITH.
BUT APPARENTLY... THE **REVERSE** IS TRUE.
TELL ME ABOUT **VENOM.**

IT'S NOT VENOM THAT'S THE PROBLEM. IT'S CARNAGE. HE'S BACK, AND HE'S...
...WELL, SYMBIOTES LEAVE A KIND OF MARKER IN HUMAN SPINES--CALLED A CODEX. ANYONE WHO'S EVER WORN A SYMBIOTE HAS ONE.
CARNAGE IS COLLECTING THEM, AND THE MORE HE HAS, THE CLOSER HE GETS TO...A KIND OF COMMUNION, I GUESS.
HE WANTS TO SUMMON THE SYMBIOTES' ALIEN GOD TO EARTH. KNULL--GOD OF THE VOID. AND IF HE GETS HERE...
THIS GUY IS NOT GOOD NEWS, BRUCE. HE'S OLDER THAN TIME. HE'S...
...HE'S COSMIC SATAN.
HMH.
YOU DON'T SAY.
"COSMIC SATAN."

THE ONE BELOW ALL.
THAT'S WHAT THAT SOUNDED LIKE TO ME.

SO I CAN'T DISCOUNT THE POSSIBILITY THAT THIS ***"KNULL"*** OF YOURS IS SOME--SOME ***FACET*** OF THE ONE BELOW ALL.
OR SOME CREATURE IT CONTROLS, SOMETHING IT'S WORKING THROUGH.

GETTING INVOLVED WITH THIS IS A **MISTAKE.**
ROSS IS BACK IN HIS GRAVE--THAT PART'S OVER. SO WE'RE **DONE.**

"**HEAVILY** INVOLVED."
THE MAGIC CODEX-EXTRACTING DOOHICKEY. LISTEN-- COULD YOU GIVE IT A LOOK OVER?
I DON'T TOTALLY **TRUST** THIS **MAKER** GUY...
I'M...NOT AS SMART AS I **WAS.** BUT I'LL DO WHAT I CAN.
ARE WE EXPECTING ANYONE ELSE HERE...?

KRAK
"JUST SOME AMAZING FRIENDS."

BRUCE. IT'S GOOD TO SEE YOU.
I...WANTED TO APOLOGIZE **PERSONALLY** FOR WHAT HAPPENED IN IOWA. NOT THE AVENGERS' FINEST HOUR.*
IT'S FINE, CAP.
THAT SAID... WE'D LIKE YOU TO COME **IN.** JUST TO **TALK** TO US.
WE **CAN** HELP YOU, BRUCE.
*EDITORS NOTE: SEE **IMMORTAL HULK #7,** TRUE BELIEVERS!

"AND YOUR **FRIENDS.**"
NICE TO MEET YOU. I'M EDDIE.
BRUCE BANNER. WE'VE ACTUALLY MET A FEW TIMES-- WE BOTH LOOKED A BIT DIFFERENT, THOUGH.
OH MAN... DID I... DID **WE...**

"...NOT NOW!"

... ALL RIGHT.

JUST SEEMS LONGER IN HERE, THAT'S ALL. WE CAN STILL REJECT THIS THING.
I'LL TEAR MY OWN SPINE OUT IF I GOTTA--
NO.

I'M WILLING TO ACCEPT HIM. WORK WITH HIM.
IF WE COMBINE OUR FORCES, WE CAN--
IT DON'T WORK THAT WAY! OPEN YOUR EYES, BANNER!
LOOK AT IT!

IT'S AN ALIEN PARASITE! IT INFECTS PEOPLE! IT USES PEOPLE!
IT DON'T GIVE A DAMN ABOUT YOU OR US OR ANYBODY ELSE! IT DOESN'T WANT US!
ALL IT WANTS IS OUR STRENGTH!

SO? HULK IS STRONGEST ONE THERE IS.
HULK HAS STRENGTH FOR ALL HULK'S FRIENDS.
AIN'T LIKE WE'RE GETTING THROUGH THIS WITHOUT A FIGHT ANYHOW.
NEW KID'S GOT MOXIE-- LET'S SEE WHAT HE CAN DO.

BANNER--LISTEN TO ME. YOU KNOW WHAT HAPPENS WHEN YOU DON'T LISTEN TO ME.
WE'RE A SYSTEM--AND THAT THING AIN'T A PART OF IT. WE LET IT IN, ALL IT'LL DO IS MESS US UP, GUM UP THE WORKS--
SORRY, HULK.

HULK IS HULK.
IT'S A MISTAKE, BANNER. WHEN THIS ALL FALLS APART, YOU JUST REMEMBER THAT.
JUST REMEMBER I TOLD YOU.

THREE VOTES TO ONE. TWO ABSTENTIONS, IF WE'RE COUNTING DORMANT ALTERS. IT'S SETTLED.
YOU'RE WITH US NOW, VENOM.

"WELCOME TO THE FAMILY."

WE ARE HULK

AL EWING
WRITER

FILIPE ANDRADE
ARTIST

CHRIS O'HALLORAN
COLORIST

TRAVIS LANHAM
LETTERER

DALE KEOWN & JASON KEITH
ABSOLUTE CARNAGE: IMMORTAL HULK CODEX VARIANT

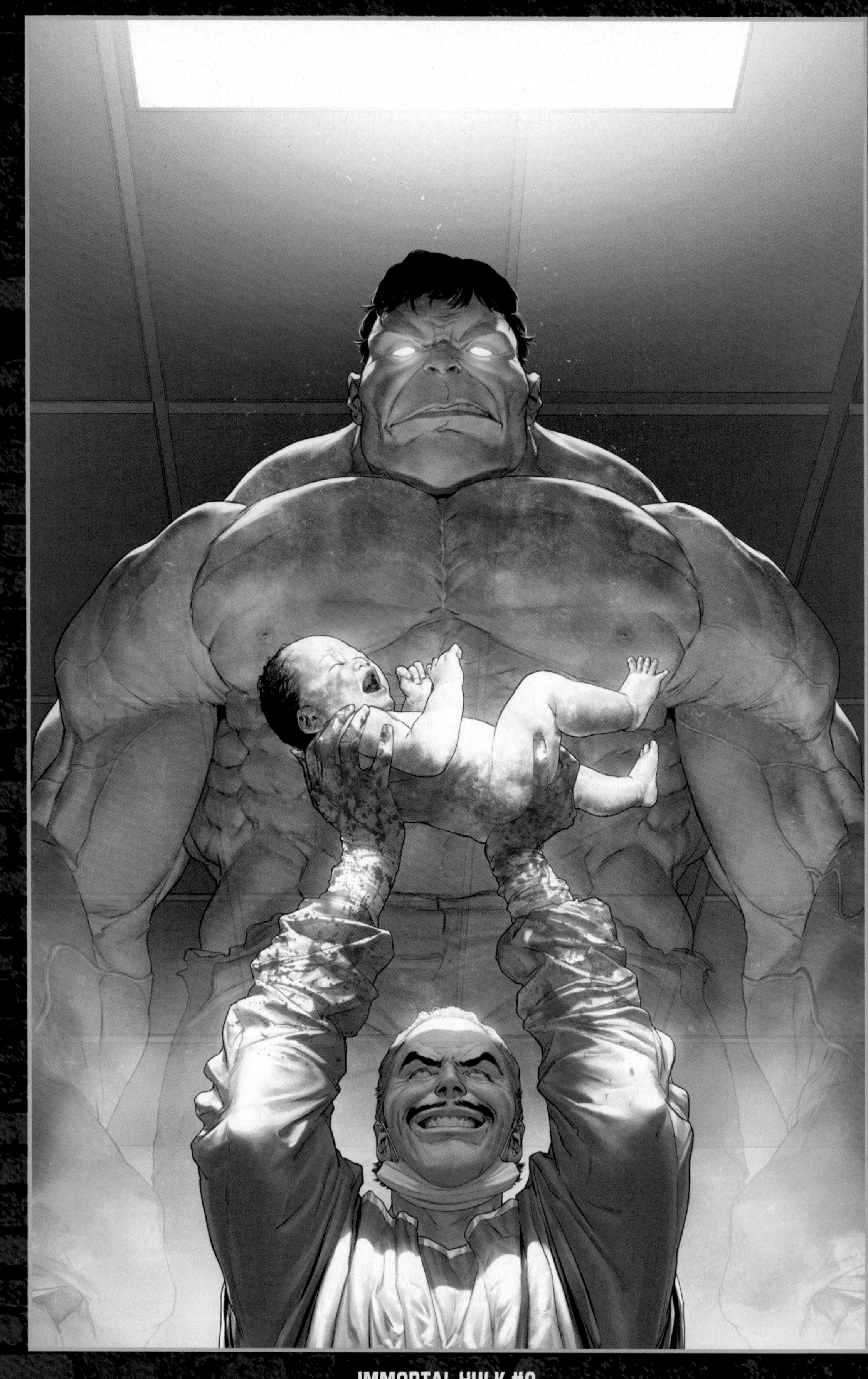

IMMORTAL HULK #0

"AND WHO SHALL REPAY HIM WHAT HE HATH DONE? YET SHALL HE BE BROUGHT TO THE GRAVE, AND SHALL REMAIN IN THE TOMB."

— JOB 21:31-32

REBECCA?
I...I THOUGHT I HEARD YOU ***SCREAMING.***
THERE WAS A ***HOSPITAL...*** YOU HAD SOME... ***DISEASE*** INSIDE YOU...
OH GOD.
NO.

NO, NO, *NO*...

REBECCA BANNER

YOU'RE NOT *DEAD*, REBECCA! YOU'RE *NOT!*

STOP IT! STOP *FAKING!*

STOP FAKING, REBECCA! GET UP OFF THE DRIVEWAY!

YOU'RE-- YOU'RE ONLY MAKING A FOOL OF YOURSELF--

DAYTON, OHIO -- A LIFETIME AGO...
OHIO GENERAL HOSPITAL
EEEEEEYAAAAGHHH
MATERNITY
WHAT'S HAPPENING TO MY WIFE?! WHY IS SHE SCREAMING?!
PLEASE, DR. BANNER! YOU'RE HURTING ME!
SOMEONE SUMMON MRS. BANNER'S OBSTETRICIAN!
TELL HIM HER HUSBAND'S GOING CRAZY!

AND SOON...
WE TOLD YOU, DR. BANNER, THAT THE BIRTH OF YOUR CHILD MIGHT BE... DIFFICULT... DUE TO THE POSITION OF THE BABY IN THE WOMB!
BUT WHY MUST MY WIFE SUFFER?

I TOLD HER I DIDN'T WANT A CHILD YET! WE BOTH WORK SO HARD WE HARDLY HAVE TIME FOR EACH OTHER AS IT IS!

HER LABOR IS THE MOST PAINFUL I'VE EVER ATTENDED. SHE IS AT GREAT RISK.
I AM RECOMMENDING THAT A CAESARIAN SECTION BE PERFORMED TO SAVE HER LIFE AND THAT OF THE CHILD.

THE CHILD? DOCTOR, MY WIFE IS THE PRIORITY!
I LOVE MY WIFE! DO WHAT YOU CAN TO SAVE HER--REGARDLESS...
LORD, WHY DIDN'T I REMEMBER TO BRING A BOTTLE WITH ME?

BILL MANTLO	MIKE MIGNOLA	JIM NOVAK	BOB SHAREN	CARL POTTS	JIM SHOOTER
STORY	ART	LETTERS	COLORS	EDITOR	EDITOR IN CHIEF

THE DECISION WAS DR. BRIAN BANNER'S.

HIS WIFE WAS IN NO SHAPE TO DECIDE ANYTHING.

HERE, MRS. BANNER! INHALE THIS!

THE ANESTHETIC GAS SWEPT REBECCA BANNER INTO SWEET OBLIVION...

SHE'S UNDER, DOCTOR!

EVERYTHING'S PROCEEDING NORMALLY NOW.

KEEP MONITORING HER LIFE-SIGNS! NOTHING IS NORMAL ABOUT THIS BIRTH!

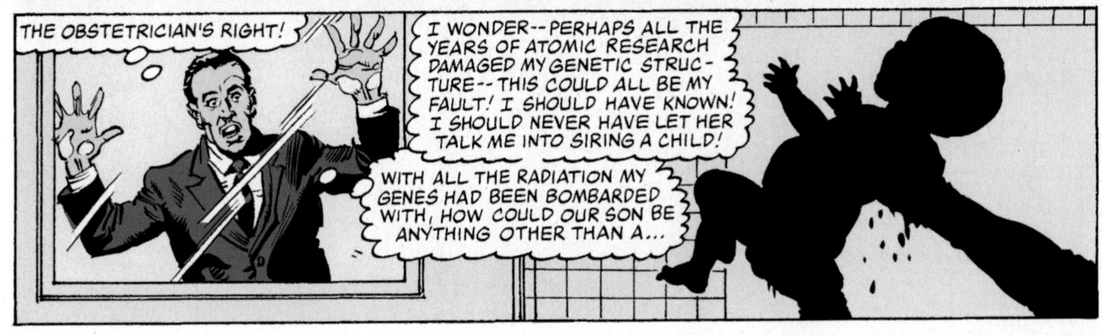

THE OBSTETRICIAN'S RIGHT!
I WONDER--PERHAPS ALL THE YEARS OF ATOMIC RESEARCH DAMAGED MY GENETIC STRUCTURE--THIS COULD ALL BE MY FAULT! I SHOULD HAVE KNOWN! I SHOULD NEVER HAVE LET HER TALK ME INTO SIRING A CHILD!
WITH ALL THE RADIATION MY GENES HAD BEEN BOMBARDED WITH, HOW COULD OUR SON BE ANYTHING OTHER THAN A...

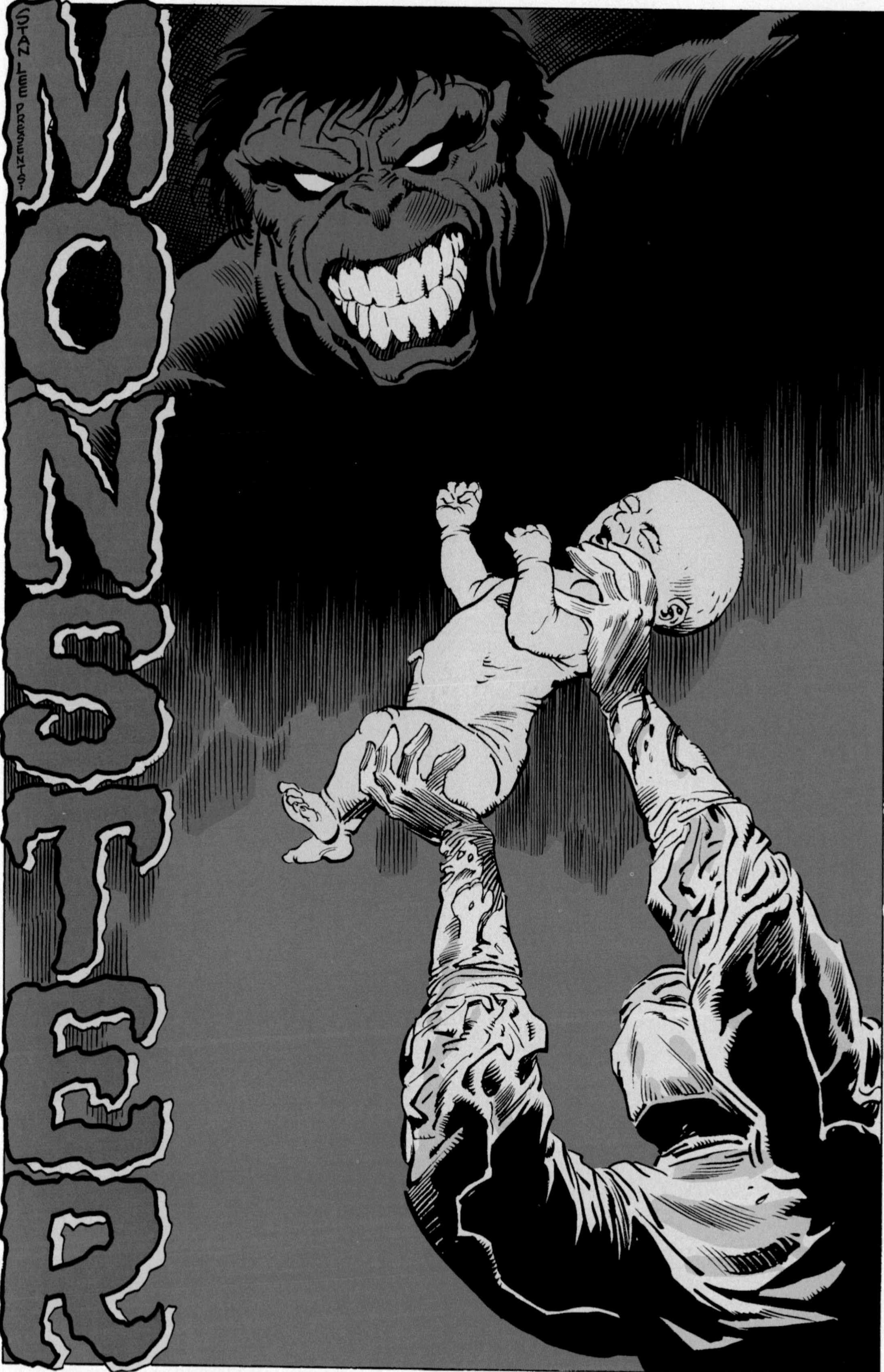
STAN LEE PRESENTS:
MONSTER

IT WAS SEVERAL MONTHS BEFORE THE BANNERS WERE ALLOWED TO BRING THEIR BABY HOME...

HOW BIG BRUCE HAS GROWN, BRIAN!
THEY HAD TO KEEP HIM IN INTENSIVE CARE, REBECCA -- TO STUDY HIM.

AND THEY FOUND NOTHING WRONG! WHY SHOULD THEY HAVE?
OUR BABY IS HAPPY, HEALTHY...

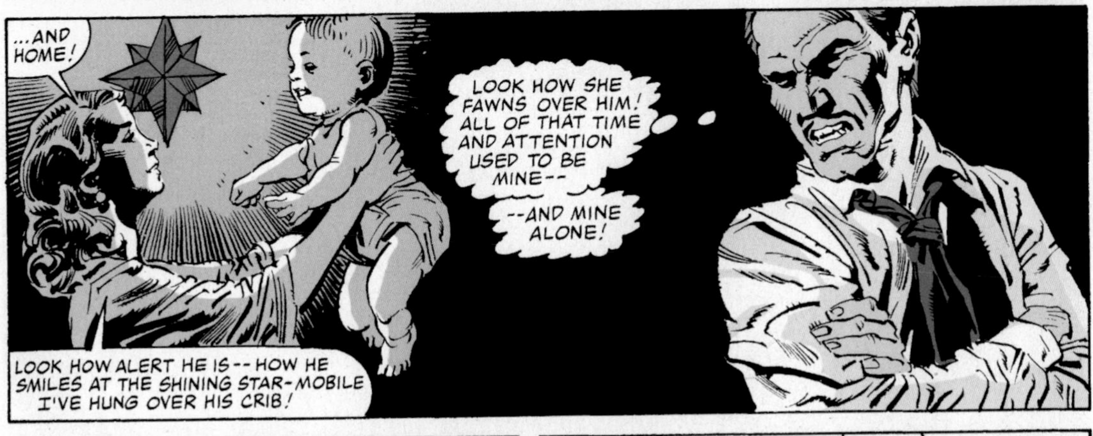
...AND HOME!
LOOK HOW ALERT HE IS--HOW HE SMILES AT THE SHINING STAR-MOBILE I'VE HUNG OVER HIS CRIB!
LOOK HOW SHE FAWNS OVER HIM! ALL OF THAT TIME AND ATTENTION USED TO BE MINE--
--AND MINE ALONE!

WHY DON'T YOU EVER HOLD OUR SON, BRIAN?
COME, REBECCA. IT'S GETTING LATE. WE'VE THAT SYMPOSIUM TO ATTEND, AND LATER DINNER WITH THE BAXTERS.
BUT BRUCE HAS ONLY JUST BEEN RETURNED TO US! CAN'T WE STAY IN AND SPEND THE NIGHT WITH HIM?

THE SYMPOSIUM IS IMPORTANT TO MY CAREER. NURSE MEACHUM WILL SIT WITH BRUCE WHILE WE'RE OUT.
I WISH...
I'M SURE DR. BANNER KNOWS BEST, MA'AM!

AND DON'T YOU WORRY! I'LL TAKE THE VERY BEST CARE OF BABY BRUCE!
THE BANNERS LEFT...
WAAAA

SHUT YOUR TRAP!
I DON'T WANT THIS JOB--I NEED THIS JOB!
BUT IF I'VE GOT TO STOOP TO MINDIN' OTHER PEOPLE'S BRATS--
--I EXPECT 'EM TO BE QUIET AND AMUSE THEM-SELVES!
HERE! YOUR MOTHER LEFT YOU THIS DOLL!

PIPE DOWN AND PLAY!
AT AN AGE WHEN OTHER CHILDREN WERE LEARNING TO LAUGH, BRUCE BANNER LEARNED LONELINESS.

WHEN HIS MOTHER WAS THERE, IT WAS DIFFERENT.
BUT HIS FATHER ALLOWED HIS MOTHER TO BE THERE SO RARELY.

INSTINCTIVELY SHUNNING HIS LOATHSOME NURSE, THE CHILD SOUGHT SOLACE IN THE PLAY-THINGS HIS MOTHER PROVIDED FOR HIM.
THE SHIMMERING STAR THAT HUNG OVER HIS CRIB, DISPELLING HIS DARKNESS...
...AND THE BELOVED DOLL STOOD SENTRY AGAINST HIS SOLITUDE.

TIME PASSED, AS TIME DOES...

IT'S CHRISTMAS EVE, GUARDIAN--OUR FOURTH CHRISTMAS EVE! EVERYBODY'S SLEEPING--MOMMY, DADDY AND MEAN OLD NURSE!
IF WE'RE REAL QUIET, NO ONE'LL CATCH US SNEAKING DOWN TO SEE THE TREE!

OH, LOOK, GUARDIAN--THAT STAR! IT USED TO HANG OVER MY CRIB! MOMMY PUT IT THERE--BUT DADDY TOOK IT AWAY!
WE'RE SCARED OF THE DARK WITHOUT IT, AREN'T WE?
BUT IT'S SHINING NOW, LIGHTING UP THE WHOLE LIVING ROOM--

--AND I'M NOT SCARED... NOT WITH YOU HERE!
MOM
BRUCE
NOW YOU SIT, OKAY?
AND LET ME KNOW IF DADDY OR NURSE SHOULD COME!

IN THE CHILD'S MIND, THE LITTLE DOLL HAD GUARDED HIM AGAINST SADNESS FOR AS LONG AS BRUCE COULD REMEMBER, HENCE THE DOLL'S NAME...
WOW! THIS BIG BOX SAYS, "FROM MOMMY!" I WONDER WHAT'S IN IT, GUARDIAN!
I-I KNOW I SHOULDN'T OPEN IT YET, BUT...

TEMPTATION PROVED TOO MUCH FOR THE LONELY FOUR YEAR OLD WHOSE CURIOSITY AND CREATIVITY WAS SO OFTEN SUPPRESSED...
SOME KIND OF BUILDING SET! I'VE NEVER SEEN ANYTHING LIKE IT...!
AND YET, BRUCE BANNER MASTERED THE INTRICACIES OF AN ERECTOR SET IN A MATTER OF MINUTES.
HE LABORED BY THE LIGHT OF A STAR...
...WHILE HIS RAG DOLL STOOD GUARD OVER HIS HAPPINESS.
THERE! IT'S DONE! I WISH MOMMY COULD SEE IT! SHE'D BE SO PROUD OF ME...!
THUMP!
GUARDIAN! WHAT HAPPENED? WHAT MADE YOU FALL...?

WHAT IS THE MEANING OF OF THIS, YOUNG MAN?!
D-DADDY! I WAS JUST BUILD-ING...!

NO CHILD YOUR AGE SHOULD BE ABLE TO BUILD SOMETHING SO INTRICATE!

NOW I UNDERSTAND! YOU MUST BE A FREAK AFTER ALL!

THE RADIATION DIDN'T AFFECT YOUR BODY -- IT'S YOUR MIND THAT IT ALTERED!

DADDY, Y-YOU'RE SCARING ME!
I SHOULD HAVE DIED YEARS AGO!

BUT IT'S NOT TOO LATE! I CAN DO IT... NOW... BEFORE YOU GROW TO MANHOOD... AND INTO AN EVEN BIGGER FREAK WHOSE UNNATURAL GENIUS MAKES YOU SUPERIOR TO WE "MERE MORTALS!"
BRIAN! WHY ARE YOU YELLING AT OUR SON?
H--HAVE YOU BEEN DRINKING AGAIN?

GO BACK TO BED, REBECCA! THAT... THAT THING ISN'T OUR "SON!"
HAVE YOU GONE MAD? I GAVE BIRTH TO BRUCE! HE GREW INSIDE MY BODY!
THE DAMAGE WAS DONE LONG BEFORE THEN!

THE FAULT WAS MINE, AND I INTEND TO CORRECT MY MISTAKE... NOW!
NO! I WON'T LET YOU HARM BRUCE--!
OHHH!
SLAP

MOMMY!
YOU MAY HAVE FOOLED YOUR MOTHER--
FWAK!
--BUT I'VE KNOWN WHAT YOU WOULD BECOME EVER SINCE THE BEGINNING!
BRUCE! BRIAN, YOU ARE INSANE! HOW COULD YOU HIT OUR CHILD--?!
CHILD? NO NORMAL CHILD, NOT THAT ONE!
HE'S SOMETHING DIFFERENT... INHUMAN!
"MY SON"--THE MONSTER!

YOU NEVER TOLD ME ABOUT YOUR WORK AT LOS ALAMOS, BRIAN. I NEVER ASKED, BUT I ALWAYS SUSPECTED THAT IT HAD SOMETHING TO DO WITH THE BOMB AND ATOMIC ENERGY.
YOU WERE EXPOSED TO SOME SORT OF RADIATION, WEREN'T YOU? YOU FEARED THAT GENETIC DAMAGE WAS DONE AND THAT IT WOULD BE HEREDITARY.
BUT THE DOCTORS CHECKED HIM THOROUGHLY ...THERE WAS NOTHING WRONG WITH HIM!
I KNOW HE'S A FREAK AND IT WAS YOU WHO WANTED A CHILD! I WANTED YOUR ATTENTION--FOR THE TWO OF US TO BE HAPPY--WE USED TO GET ALONG SO WELL! IF ONLY YOU HADN'T INSISTED ON HAVING A CHILD!

I HEARD... VOICES... DR. BANNER, IS ANYTHING WRONG?
MY WIFE AND I ARE... TALKING... NURSE MEACHUM. PLEASE TAKE BRUCE BACK TO HIS ROOM.

AND SO, RATHER THAN HURT ME, YOU ALLOWED ME TO BEAR A CHILD--
--WHOM YOU'VE HATED EVER SINCE!
YES, BRIAN, WE HAVE MUCH TO TALK ABOUT--

--BUT NOT IN FRONT OF BRUCE!
THERE WERE SO MANY THINGS BRUCE BANNER COULDN'T UNDERSTAND...

...LIKE WHY HE NEVER SAW HIS MOTHER SMILE AGAIN.

YEARS LATER...
SCIENCE HIGH SCHOOL

BANNER'S ALWAYS WORKING!
EVEN IN THIS SCHOOL FULL OF GIFTED STUDENTS, BANNER MAKES THE REST OF US LOOK LIKE PIKERS!
HE NEVER EVEN TALKS TO HIS CLASSMATES!
MAYBE HE THINKS HE'S TOO SMART?

THAT'S WHY I'VE ASKED YOU TO COME IN, MRS. DRAKE. YOUR NEPHEW IS BRILLIANT. NO INTELLIGENCE TEST HAS BEEN DEVELOPED TO ADEQUATELY MEASURE BRUCE'S I.Q..
BUT HE SHUNS HIS FELLOW STUDENTS EVEN AS HE IS SHUNNED BY THEM. HE HAS NO FRIENDS. HE CARES FOR NOTHING BUT HIS STUDIES.
BRUCE HAD A... DIFFICULT... CHILDHOOD, HEADMASTER.

I KNEW THAT DR. BANNER HAD KILLED HIS WIFE...
YES... MY SISTER.
IT WAS VERY BAD FOR BRUCE A LONG TIME BEFORE THAT TRAGEDY AS WELL.

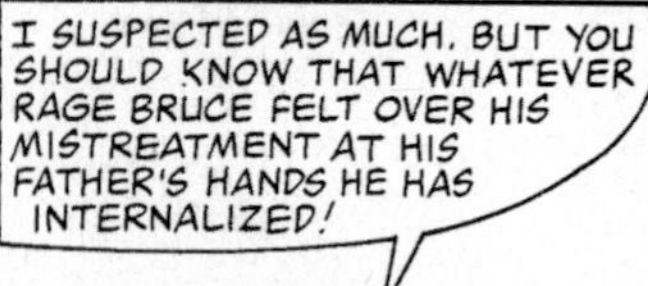
I SUSPECTED AS MUCH. BUT YOU SHOULD KNOW THAT WHATEVER RAGE BRUCE FELT OVER HIS MISTREATMENT AT HIS FATHER'S HANDS HE HAS INTERNALIZED!

"I DREAD THE DAY WHEN HE FINALLY LETS IT OUT!"
THIS SHOULD SHAKE YOU UP A LITTLE BIT, BIG BRAIN!

WHAT'S THAT STRANGE SIZZLING SOUND--? GOOD HEAVENS! MY EXPERIMENT, SEETHING, BOILING OVER!
BUT...THAT'S IMPOSSIBLE!
SOMETHING WRONG, BANNER?

NO! MY CALCULATIONS WERE ALL CORRECT! THERE IS NO WAY THE CHEMICALS I MIXED COULD HAVE INTERACTED--

BANNER! IS THIS YOUR IDEA OF A JOKE?!!

IMPOSSIBLE! COULDN'T... SHOULDN'T HAVE HAPPENED!

NO, MR. THAYER. IT WASN'T MY IDEA AT ALL.

I'D EXPECTED YOU TO BE MORE MATURE, BANNER. YOU NEVER SEEMED THE TYPE TO ENGAGE IN ATTENTION-GETTING PRANKS.

THAT'S THE TROUBLE WITH EGG-HEADS!

YOU NEVER KNOW WHEN THEY'LL CRACK!

AND LATER STILL...
SO, YOU ARE HERE?
WHERE ELSE SHOULD I BE, "FATHER..."

...OTHER THAN BY MY MOTHER'S SIDE ON THE ANNIVERSARY OF HER MURDER.
REBECCA BANNER
MAY SHE REST IN PEACE

I HAD HEARD THEY'D LET YOU OUT OF THE MENTAL HOS-PITAL--INSANITY CURED AND ON GOOD BEHAVIOR, WASN'T IT?

THEY DIDN'T ALLOW ME TO ATTEND THE FUNERAL!

YOU'VE GOT SOME NERVE COMING HERE TODAY!
BACK OFF, MONSTER!

MONSTER? YOU STILL SUFFER THAT DELUSION?!
TEMPORARY INSANITY THE COURT CALLED IT.
YOU FOOLED THE JURY, BUT YOU DIDN'T FOOL ME!
YOU TORTURED US FOR YEARS!

AND WHEN MOTHER FINALLY TRIED TO ESCAPE YOUR MADNESS, YOU MURDERED HER!!
YOUR MOTHER WAS A FOOL! SHE KNEW WHAT YOU WERE, YET SHE ALLOWED YOU TO GROW TO MANHOOD WITH THE EVIL STILL INSIDE YOU!
THE ONLY "EVIL" WAS YOURS, FATHER, WHEN YOU CURSED YOUR SON AND KILLED YOUR WIFE!

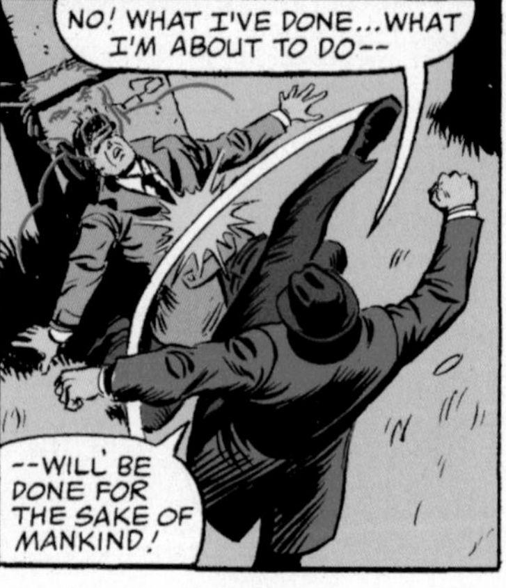
NO! WHAT I'VE DONE...WHAT I'M ABOUT TO DO--
--WILL BE DONE FOR THE SAKE OF MANKIND!

AND I KNEW YOU WERE A MONSTER BUT THE WORLD WOULDN'T BELIEVE ME!
I KNOW YOU'RE A MUTANT!

I'VE READ REPORTS OF OTHERS LIKE YOU--
--BENT ON HUMANITY'S DESTRUCTION!

BUT NOW THAT I'VE FOUND YOU AGAIN I'LL REVEAL YOU TO THE WORLD! ONCE YOUR WORK IS SCRUTINIZED, THEY'LL KNOW THAT NO HUMAN INTELLECT COULD MAKE THE SCIENTIFIC LEAPS YOU'VE MADE!
AND ONCE THEY REALIZE THAT YOU'RE NOT HUMAN, THEY'LL PREVENT YOU FROM EVER USING YOUR RADIATION-SPAWNED GENIUS TO EDGE HUMANITY ASIDE!

MOTHER WAS RIGHT, FATHER! YOU'RE MAD!
THERE'S NOTHING WRONG WITH ME! I MAY BE EXCEPTIONALLY SMART, BUT THAT'S MY GIFT... NOT YOUR MISTAKE!
IF I WAS A MUTANT ANY LATENT "POWERS" WOULD HAVE SHOWN THEMSELVES IN EARLY ADOLESCENCE--I'VE ALWAYS BEEN SMART.

SO SPREAD YOUR INSANE, SLANDEROUS STORIES, FATHER! WHAT DOES IT MATTER WHAT YOU OR OTHERS THINK ABOUT ME OR MY WORK NOW? YOU'VE ALREADY TAKEN FROM ME THE ONLY PERSON I'VE EVER LOVED ...THE ONLY ONE WHO EVER LOVED ME!
IN ALL MY YEARS OF DARKNESS, SHE SHONE LIKE A STAR!

BUT THINKING OF YOU ALWAYS DIMMED HER LUMINESCENCE, FATHER!

I'D HOPED TO MAKE HER FORGET YOU--
--BY MAKING HER PROUD OF ME!

BUT NOW HER LIFE... AND HER LIGHT... ARE GONE!

AT EASE, CORPORAL... AT LEAST WHILE MY ***FATHER'S*** NOT AROUND!

DR. BANNER? I'M ***BETTY ROSS.***

WELL! I'D HEARD A LOT ABOUT GENERAL THADDEUS "THUNDERBOLT" ROSS BEFORE I CAME HERE--

--BUT I SEE THEY CENSORED THE ***BEST*** THINGS FROM MY BRIEFING!

I APPRECIATE THE COMPLIMENT, DR. BANNER...

CALL ME BRUCE.

...BUT YOU'D BETTER NOT LET DADDY HEAR YOU TALK LIKE THAT. HE FROWNS ON MY PRESENCE HERE ON AN ISOLATED ARMY BASE SURROUNDED BY SOLDIERS AND SCIENTISTS!

THEN WHY ARE YOU HERE, MISS ROSS?

BETTY.

BECAUSE DADDY'S HERE. HE MAY GROWL AN AWFUL LOT, BUT I DO LOVE HIM.

WHO'S THAT?

MY MOTHER. SHE'S DEAD.

AND THIS?

JUST AN OLD DOLL. I MEANT TO THROW IT OUT--

FRAGILE

--BUT SOME-HOW FORGOT TO!
IT'S NICE TO HOLD ONTO OLD THINGS, OLD MEMORIES!
IS IT? I NEVER THOUGHT SO.
BETTY!
OH, HELLO, DADDY!
I WAS JUST WELCOMING DR. BANNER TO DESERT BASE!
I EXPECT MY AIDE DE CAMP TO PER-FORM THAT FUNCTION, NOT MY DAUGH-TER! STOP DISTRACTING THE MAN, BETTY, AND LET HIM GET TO WORK!
SURELY HE'S ALLOWED TO UNPACK FIRST, FATHER...
BLAST IT! THIS IS A MILITARY BASE, NOT A REST RANCH! THE PENTAGON GAVE ME A SCHEDULE, AND I INTEND TO STICK TO IT!

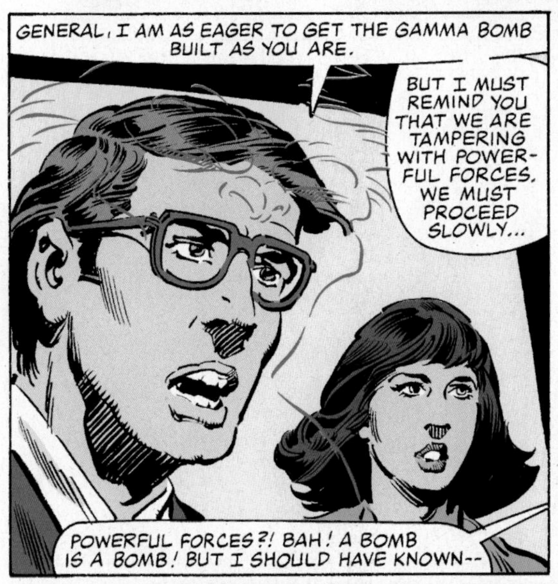
GENERAL, I AM AS EAGER TO GET THE GAMMA BOMB BUILT AS YOU ARE.
BUT I MUST REMIND YOU THAT WE ARE TAMPERING WITH POWER-FUL FORCES. WE MUST PROCEED SLOWLY...
POWERFUL FORCES?! BAH! A BOMB IS A BOMB! BUT I SHOULD HAVE KNOWN--

--THAT THEY'D SEND ME A SIMPERING CIVILIAN INSTEAD OF A MILITARY MAN TO COMPLETE THIS PROJECT!
I KNEW YOUR FATHER AT LOS ALAMOS, BANNER! NOW THERE WAS A REAL MAN--!
THE JURY THAT FOUND HIM NOT GUILTY BY REASON OF INSANITY OF KILLING MY MOTHER HAD ANOTHER WORD FOR HIM, GENERAL...

...MURDERER.
OH, NO!
WELL, PERHAPS HE WAS TOO DEDICATED TO HIS WORK! MIGHT HAVE MADE HIM UNSTABLE! THAT'S ANOTHER REASON I'M WORRIED ABOUT YOU!
THIS PROJECT IS TOO BLASTED IMPORTANT TO BE JEAPORDIZED BY SOME MEWLING MILKSOP ALL TORN UP OVER THE PROBLEMS OF HIS PAST!

I WANT A **BOMB**, BANNER!

AND I DON'T WANT ANYTHING GETTING IN THE WAY OF YOUR BUILDING ME ONE!

"JUST AN OLD DOLL," BANNER HAD CALLED IT BEEN WITH HIM SINCE HE WAS A BABY...

...PROTECTED HIM IN TIMES OF TROUBLE, SOOTHED HIS SOUL IN HIS TIME OF PAIN.

A GIFT FROM HIS MOTHER...

DON'T MIND DAD, BRUCE!

...HIS MOTHER WHO HAD SHONE LIKE A STAR!

EVER SINCE HE WAS NICKNAMED "THUNDERBOLT" ROSS HE'S TRIED TO LIVE UP TO IT!

I...THANK YOU, BETTY.

BUT YOUR FATHER NEEDN'T WORRY. I'LL BUILD HIM HIS **GAMMA BOMB**.
I KNOW YOU WILL, BRUCE.
HRMMMPHH! IT'S DING-DONG WELL ABOUT TIME!

YES, IT'S ALL ABOUT TIME.
T-MINUS SIXTY MINUTES AND HOLDING!

LISTEN, BANNER! YOU MUST TELL ME THE SECRET OF HARNESSING GAMMA RAYS!

IT ISN'T RIGHT THAT ONE MAN SHOULD HORDE SUCH KNOWLEDGE! SHOULD ANYTHING HAPPEN TO YOU...!
THE GAMMA FORMULAE ARE LOCKED SAFELY INSIDE MY COTTAGE, IGOR!
I'LL RELEASE THEM TO THE GOVERNMENT IF AND WHEN OUR TEST BLAST TODAY IS SUCCESSFUL.

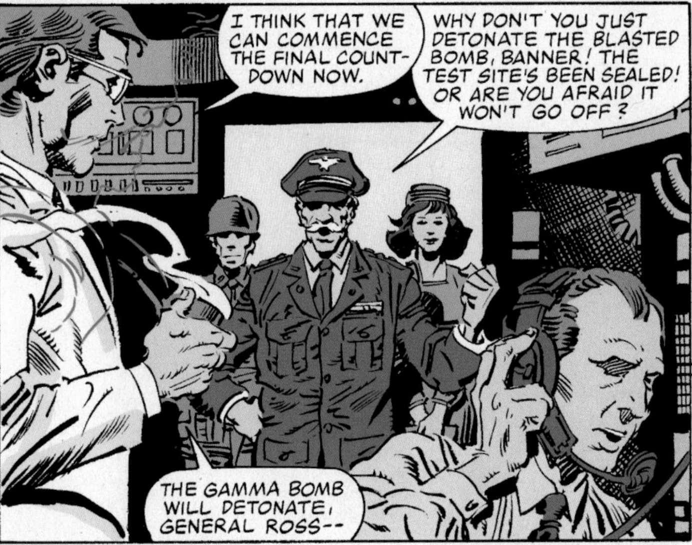
I THINK THAT WE CAN COMMENCE THE FINAL COUNT-DOWN NOW.
WHY DON'T YOU JUST DETONATE THE BLASTED BOMB, BANNER! THE TEST SITE'S BEEN SEALED! OR ARE YOU AFRAID IT WON'T GO OFF?
THE GAMMA BOMB WILL DETONATE, GENERAL ROSS--

--ALTHOUGH IN DAYS TO COME WE MAY ALL WISH IT HADN'T.

BANNER'S MISGIVINGS ABOUT THE AWESOME FORCES HE WAS TAMPERING WITH WERE NOT SHARED BY HIS ASSISTANT, IGOR SKLAR...
MY COUNTRY WOULD PAY A FORTUNE FOR THIS BOMB!

BANNER SAID THE PLANS WERE IN HIS COTTAGE! NO ONE ELSE KNOWS THAT! IF I CAN ONLY PREVENT HIM FROM RETURNING TO CLAIM THEM...!
IN A FEW SECONDS WE'LL LEARN WHAT HAPPENS WHEN GAMMA RAYS ARE UNLEASHED!

WAIT! WHAT'S THAT? GOOD LORD, IT'S A BOY--A TEENAGER! HE'S DRIVING INTO THE TEST AREA!

IGOR! DELAY THE COUNTDOWN UNTIL I CAN GET TO THAT BOY! HURRY, MAN! EVERY SECOND COUNTS!
SURE...

WHAT A STROKE OF LUCK! ALL I HAVE TO DO IS KEEP MY FINGER OFF THE "HOLD" BUTTON--

--AND IT'LL BE THE END OF BRUCE BANNER!

YOU! GET OUT OF THERE! YOU'RE IN A FORBIDDEN TEST ZONE!
COOL IT, MAN! THE KIDS BET ME I WOULDN'T HAVE NERVE ENOUGH TO SNEAK PAST THE GUARDS!

MEANWHILE, AT THE COMMAND BUNKER, NO ONE HAVING BEEN TOLD TO DELAY THE FIRING, A FINGER MOVES CLOSER TOWARDS THE FATAL BUTTON!
FIVE
FOUR
THREE...

HEY! WHAT'RE YA TRYIN' TO DO? MAKE THE GANG THINK I'M CHICKEN?
COME ON, YOU FOOL! WE'VE GOT TO GET INTO THE PROTECTIVE TRENCH BEFORE THE BOMB GOES OFF!
BOMB?
...TWO
ONE...

...FIRE!

ALTHOUGH MANY MILES FROM BOMB ZERO, BRUCE BANNER WAS BATHED IN THE FULL FORCE OF THE MYSTERIOUS GAMMA RAYS!
HE SCREAMED, BUT NO ONE HEARD HIM...
...JUST AS NO ONE HAD HEARD HIS SILENT SCREAMING ALL HIS LONELY LIFE!

THE AWESOME FORCES OF GAMMA RADIATION WERE RELEASED THAT DAY!

BUT SO WAS THE LONG PENT-UP RAGE LOCKED IN-SIDE A LOVELORN CHILD...

...DOOMED FROM CHILDHOOD TO BECOME THAT WHICH HIS FATHER HAD ALWAYS FEARED HE WOULD BECOME!
MORE THAN A MAN!

A MONSTER!
BUT THAT WAS THEN.

THE TIME: NOW. THE PLACE: AN INTERDIMENSIONAL INTERSECTION CALLED THE CROSSROADS. THE PLAYERS: AN EXILED HULK AND THREE BEINGS WHO HAVE STEPPED FORTH FROM THE DEEPEST RECESSES OF THE BEHEMOTH'S BRUTE BRAIN...
WE THREE-- GUARDIAN GLOW AND GOBLIN-- ARE ALL THAT REMAINS OF THE CURSED CHILD WHO CAME INTO THE WORLD AS BRUCE BANNER!
I REPRESENT HIS INSTINCT FOR SELF-PRESERVATION... AN INSTINCT WHICH FAILED HIM!
AND I REPRESENT HIS ABILITY TO REASON...
...HIS BRILLIANCE AND HIS LOGIC WHICH LED TO HIS BUILDING OF THE GAMMA BOMB, THE VERY FORCE THAT SEALED HIS FATE!
ME, I'M BANNER'S RAGE, LOCKED UP ALL THOSE LONELY YEARS AN' JUST WAITIN' T'BE SET FREE!
FUNNY THING IS, WHEN I FINALLY GOT THE CHANCE, BANNER TOOK A POWDER... T'BE REPLACED BY THE HULK!
YES! HURT SO OFTEN AS A CHILD, BRUCE BANNER LEARNED TO LIVE INSIDE HIMSELF, NEVER TO LET US-- HIS REASON, HIS RAGE, AND HIS DESIRE FOR SURVIVAL-- OUT! PERHAPS HE MIGHT HAVE, GIVEN TIME, GIVEN HELP...
BUT THEN THE GAMMA BOMB TOOK THE MAN MOLDED FROM A TWISTED CHILD AND TRANSFORMED HIM INTO THE VERY MONSTER HIS FATHER HAD ALWAYS PREDICTED HE'D BECOME!
AS YOU SAID, GUARDIAN, SUCH A FATE WAS INEVITABLE, PREORDAINED, GIVEN BRUCE BANNER'S PERCEPTION OF HIMSELF SINCE BIRTH AS A MONSTER!
HIS DADDY DID THAT TO HIM! HIS DADDY-- THE GREATEST MONSTER OF ALL!
BUT BANNER KNOWS US NOW, KNOWS WE'VE ALWAYS BEEN INSIDE O' HIM AN' ALWAYS WILL BE THERE T'HELP HIM FACE AN' MAYBE SOMEDAY OVERCOME HIS FATE!
"THE TRUTH MAY NOT MAKE HIM HAPPY, BUT AT LEAST NOW HE KNOWS HE CAN'T ESCAPE BEIN' WHAT HE IS SHORT O' DYIN'! AN' THAT MEANS HE'S READY T'COME OUT FROM HIDIN' INSIDE THE HULK AN' RECLAIM HIS LIFE AGAIN!"
AND THAT IS EXACTLY WHAT BRUCE BANNER DOES...

...ALTHOUGH IT TAKES HIM SOME TIME TO COME TO GRIPS WITH THE FACT THAT HE HAS BEEN REBORN AFTER SO DESPERATELY DESIRING DEATH. RELEASE FROM THE NIGHTMARE OF HIS EXISTENCE AS ALTER-EGO OF THE INCREDIBLE HULK IS WHAT HE DESIRED. BUT, THEN, TIME IS ALL THERE IS AT THE CROSSROADS!

THE TRIADS' PARTING GIFT OF REMEMBRANCE IS AN UNAPPRECIATED PRESENT.

SO I'M ALIVE AGAIN! MAYBE THAT'S WRONG! MAYBE I NEVER DIED! I THOUGHT I HAD! I WANTED TO BE DEAD SO THAT I COULD BE FREE OF THE HULK AND HE FREE OF ME!

BUT IT FIGURES! MY LIFE HAS BEEN A CURSE FROM THE VERY BEGINNING! WHY SHOULD I EXPECT IT TO CHANGE NOW?
WHY SHOULD I EVER HAVE HOPED TO BE ANYTHING OTHER THAN WHAT MY FATHER MADE ME?
NEVER A MAN LIKE OTHER MEN, IN CONTROL OF THEIR DESTINY, ABLE TO DREAM!
NEVER ANYTHING BUT... A MONSTER!

BRUCE.
LITTLE BRUCE. THE MONSTER.
HE DID THIS.

GREW INSIDE HER, LIKE THE CANCER HE WAS. PUSHED HER AWAY FROM ME.
HE KNEW WHAT HE WAS DOING.
HE KNEW WHAT I'D...

KRISHH

HE KNEW. THAT HIDEOUS BRAIN OF HIS... HE KNEW.
EVERY STEP OF THE WAY, HE--

HEY!
THAT'S SOMEONE'S FINAL RESTING PLACE, BUDDY!

LET'S HAVE A LITTLE RESPECT FOR THE DEAD, SHALL WE?
GOD--
HA! NO, LET'S NOT PRETEND I'M HIM.
QUITE THE REVERSE...
NO, I MEAN--YOU STARTLED ME--
I STARTLED YOU? YOU'RE ON MY TURF, FRIEND.
AND MAKING AN UNGODLY MESS OF IT, I MIGHT ADD.
LOOK, IF YOU MEAN THIS TRASH SOMEONE LEFT ON MY WIFE'S GRAVE--
IT WAS ALREADY HERE WHEN...
WHEN I...
WHAT... WHAT IS THAT?
ON THE GRAVE.
Y'KNOW... THERE WAS ANOTHER GUY WHO TENDED THESE PLOTS ONCE. HE HAD A STORY ABOUT THIS.
HOW'D IT GO AGAIN...?

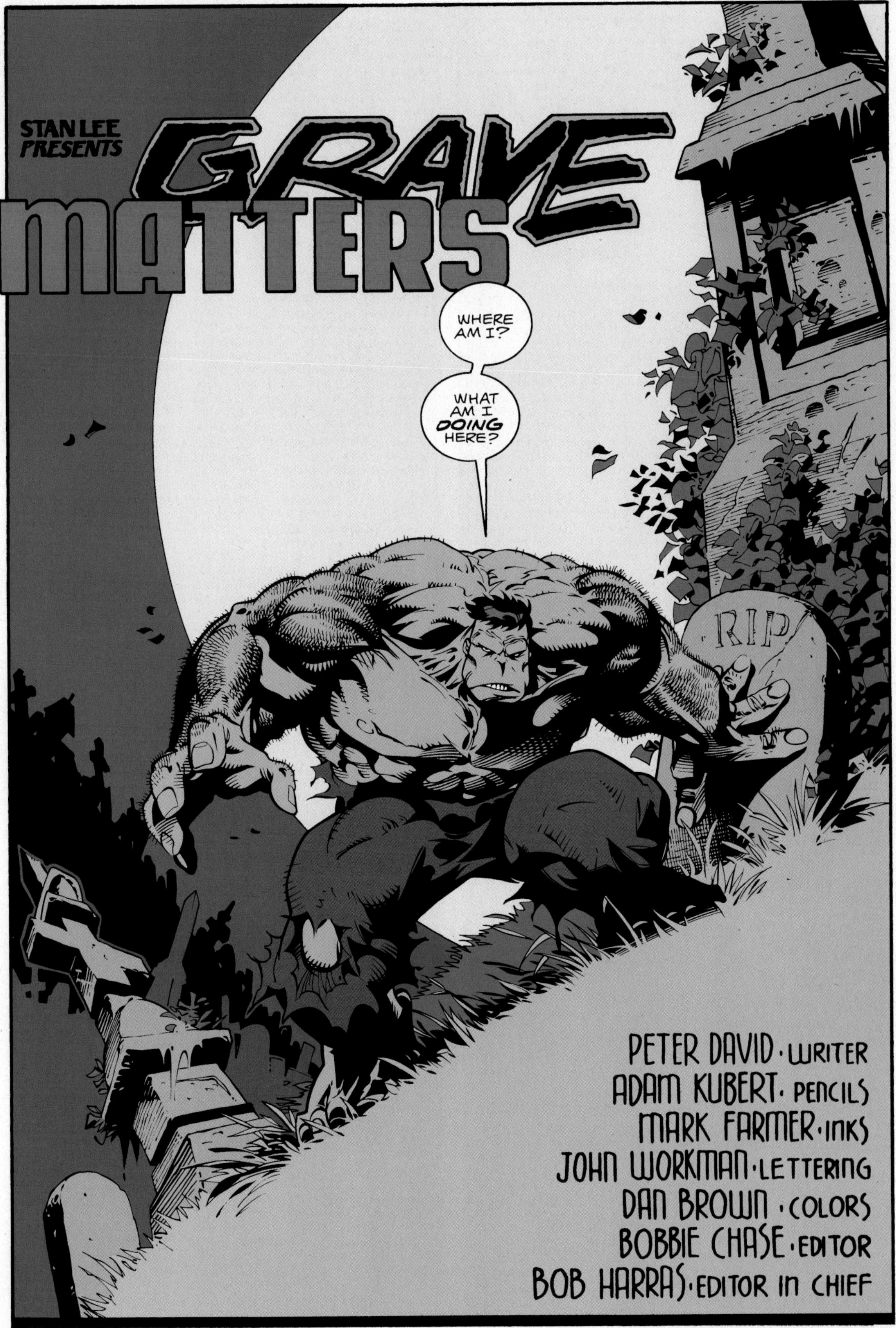
STAN LEE PRESENTS
GRAVE MATTERS
WHERE AM I?
WHAT AM I DOING HERE?
RIP
PETER DAVID · WRITER
ADAM KUBERT · PENCILS
MARK FARMER · INKS
JOHN WORKMAN · LETTERING
DAN BROWN · COLORS
BOBBIE CHASE · EDITOR
BOB HARRAS · EDITOR IN CHIEF

HUNH. THOUGHT I HEARD DIGGING.

YOU.
WHERE IS THIS PLACE?

AH! I WAS WONDERING WHEN YOU'D GET HERE!
SO... WHAT'S THE LAST THING YOU REMEMBER?

COLLAPSING.
RIGHT. IN THE SAVAGE LAND. AND NOW YOU'RE EN ROUTE TO NEW YORK.
IS... THIS A DREAM?
NOPE. A STORY... AND A TRUE ONE... ALL ABOUT YOU.

AND YOU'LL ...TELL IT?
ME? NAH! I HAVEN'T TOLD ONE OF YOUR STORIES IN AGES.
BUT DON'T WORRY! I HAVE...

...HELP!
SNAP!

HURRY! WE'RE ON!
FINALLY, A CALL TO ACTION!
PLACES, PEOPLE, PLACES!
AND NOW STAN LEE PRESENTS (AS I MODESTLY LIKE TO SHOUT)...
...A MEMORY PLAY WE LIKE TO CALL...
...THE DEATH...
...OF BRIAN...
THE DEATH OF BRIAN BANNER
...BANNER!
...OR.., BRUCE AND HIS FATHER FIGURES!
NO! GO AWAY! DON'T WANT TO HEAR THIS!
TOO LATE, MEAN GREEN!

YOU'VE PUT IT OFF LONG ENOUGH. YOU'VE HEARD BITS AND PIECES OF IT.
NOW IT'S TIME TO HEAR THE WHOLE THING, SO SETTLE *DOWN*, BIG GUY !

KIRBY THEATER
OKAY! ONCE UPON A TIME... THERE WAS A YOUNG MAN NAMED...
THE DEATH OF BRIAN BANNER

...ROBERT BRUCE!
YOU HAVE BLED WITH *WALLACE!* NOW BLEED WITH *ME!*
THE DEATH

NOT *THAT* ROBERT BRUCE, CHEESEHEAD! **ROBERT BRUCE BANNER!**
FWiiiiiiP!!!
CAN'T GET ANY DECENT HELP THESE DAYS.
THE DEATH

NOW, ROBERT BRUCE WAS JUST OUT OF COLLEGE AND ALREADY HAD A REP FOR BRILLIANCE. SO MUCH SO THAT IT HAD ATTRACTED THE ATTENTION OF THE MILITARY,
AND A GENTLEMAN WAS SENT TO MEET HIM.
HI, MOM.
A GENT NAMED... THUNDERBOLT ROSS!

FOR YOUNG BRUCE HAD A NOTION FOR A BOMB TO END ALL BOMBS. HE CALLED IT THE GAMMA BOMB.
AHEM! I SAID, "HE CALLED IT...

"...THE GAMMA BOMB!"
GAMMA BOMB

AND ROSS WAS THERE TO FIND OUT ALL ABOUT IT.

SO YOU SEE, GENERAL, THE GAMMA BOMB HAS POTENTIAL TO BE A TREMENDOUS FORCE FOR GOOD.
IF IT'S IN OUR HANDS, BANNER, THAT *MAKES* IT GOOD.
BASICALLY, IT FLIP-FLOPS THE NEUTRON BOMB. INSTEAD OF DESTROYING PEOPLE AND LEAVING PROPERTY, THE GAMMA BOMB WOULD DESTROY PROPERTY--METAL, BRICKS--WHILE SPARING LIVES.

IMAGINE AN ENEMY FINDING ITSELF BEREFT OF GUNS, TANKS, ARMAMENT. OR SURGICAL STRIKES DESTROYING MILITARY TARGETS AND SPARING SOLDIERS AND CIVILIANS.
TAP TAP TAP
LOOK, SON, I...

DON'T CALL ME "SON."
I'M NOT MUCH FOR BEING PATERNAL, BUT MY ORDERS WERE TO GO EASY ON YOU. *DEVIL* TAKE IT.

BOTTOM LINE, I DON'T NEED SOME NAMBY-PAMBY FEEL-GOOD "SAFE" WEAPON. I NEED SOMETHING TO PUT THE FEAR OF GOD INTO THE ENEMY.
THE FEAR OF *GOD*, GENERAL, OR THE FEAR OF *YOU?*
SAME DIFFERENCE.
THEY CALL ME "THUNDERBOLT," BANNER, BECAUSE WHEN I'M ANGRY...

...IT'S LIKE ZEUS THROWING **THUNDERBOLTS** FROM ON HIGH.

REMIND ME TO BE IMPRESSED, GENERAL.

THE GOVERNMENT WANTS YOU TO CREATE A LOCALIZED, ***DE-STRUCTIVE*** BOMB. YOU'LL BE PAID FAR MORE THAN IN THE PRIVATE SECTOR OR AS A TEACHER.

QUESTION IS, ARE YOU MAN ENOUGH TO TAKE THE CONTRACT?

MAN ENOUGH OR ***SOUL-LESS*** ENOUGH?

EXCUSE ME.
YES, HELLO.
YES, THIS IS DOCTOR BANNER.

BRUCE, THIS IS...
...THIS IS YOUR DAD.

I DON'T *WANT* TO SEE HIM ...OR HEAR ABOUT HIM.

I'M NOT *SURPRISED!* WHY, THE LAST PLACE YOU SAW HIM WAS A PLACE JUST LIKE THIS!
BRIAN BANNER, THE MAN WHO KILLED YOUR MOM ...THE MAN YOU TRIED TO COVER FOR AT THE TRIAL...
KA-ZAR

ALMOST WORKED, TOO...UNTIL HE WAS OVERHEARD GLOATING ABOUT HOW HE'D BROW-BEAT YOU INTO LYING.
WHACK
WHACK

REMEMBER THAT DAY?
REMEMBER?

REMEMBER THAT I'LL GET YOU! YOU LITTLE MONSTER! YOU CREATURE, YOU... YOU THING!
I'LL GET YOU! I SWEAR!
BRUCE, IT'S... IT'S GOOD TO SEE YOU, SON.

YOU'RE RELEASING HIM? YOU CAN'T BE SERIOUS.
HE'S HARDLY PERFECT, DOCTOR BANNER, BUT WHICH OF US IS?
HE'S BEEN WITH US NEARLY FIFTEEN YEARS, AND WE BELIEVE HE'S FINALLY CAPABLE OF FUNCTIONING IN SOCIETY.

HE'S DANGEROUS! A SOCIOPATH... A MURDERER!
SON... I... I WAS SICK. I ADMIT IT. AND I'VE SPENT YEARS COPING WITH THAT.

BUT THROUGH YEARS OF THERAPY... MEDICATION... I'M THE MAN YOUR DEAR MOTHER FELL IN LOVE WITH AGAIN.
TOO BAD SHE'S NOT ALIVE TO SEE IT.
I DON'T BELIEVE YOU, FATHER.

BRUCE, I'VE... I'VE NOWHERE ELSE TO GO, NO ONE ELSE TO TURN TO.
PLEASE... HELP ME.

DON'T REMEMBER ANY OF THIS...
HEY, OF COURSE YOU DON'T. THE PART OF YOU THAT WAS BRUCE BANNER SUPPRESSED THE MEMORY.

BUT WITH HIS INFLUENCE GONE, THINGS ARE COMING BACK TO YOU... THINGS LONG BURIED.
Y'KNOW, IN YOUR OWN WAY, YOUR MENTAL ACUITY IS AS SKETCHY AS YOUR OLD MAN'S. YOU'VE BLOCKED OUT YOUR TIME WITH HIM AT THE MENTAL INSTITUTION. ALL YOU REMEMBER...
...IS THIS.

WHAT I'VE DONE... WHAT I'M ABOUT TO DO... WILL BE DONE FOR THE SAKE OF MANKIND!
AND I KNEW YOU WERE A MONSTER, BUT THE WORLD WOULDN'T BELIEVE ME! I KNOW YOU'RE A MUTANT!
R.I.P.
REBECCA BANNER
THE "FIRST" TIME YOU SAW YOUR FATHER SINCE HE KILLED YOUR MOM...
...AND THE LAST TIME BEFORE HIS OWN DEATH.
THE DEATH

I'VE READ REPORTS OF OTHERS LIKE YOU, BENT ON HUMANITY'S DESTRUCTION! BUT NOW THAT I'VE FOUND YOU AGAIN, I'LL REVEAL YOU TO THE WORLD!
ONCE YOUR WORK IS SCRUTINIZED, THEY'LL KNOW THAT NO HUMAN INTELLECT COULD MAKE THE SCIENTIFIC LEAPS YOU'VE MADE!
HOP!
THE DEATH

AND ONCE THEY REALIZE THAT YOU'RE NOT HUMAN, THEY'LL PREVENT YOU FROM EVER USING YOUR RADIATION-SPAWNED GENIUS TO EDGE HUMANITY ASIDE!
MOTHER WAS RIGHT, FATHER! YOU'RE MAD!

HE WASN'T JUST MAD. HE WAS HACKED OFF.
IS THIS HOW IT HAPPENED, HULK? IS IT?
THERE'S NOTHING WRONG WITH ME! I MAY BE EXCEPTIONALLY SMART, BUT THAT'S MY GIFT ...NOT YOUR MISTAKE!

YES. THAT'S WHAT HAPPENED.

IT'S... GOOD OF YOU TO TAKE ME IN, SON. IT'S JUST FOR A SHORT WHILE, I SWEAR.
I TRY TO BE A MAN OF REASON. COMPASSIO IN SHOR YOUR OPPO
BUT IF THAT'S THE ONE AND ONLY TIME YOU SAW YOUR FATHER... HOW DO YOU EXPLAIN THIS, THEN...?
WOLVERINES
WOLVERINES

IT'S... GOOD OF YOU TO TAKE ME IN, SON. IT'S JUST FOR A SHORT WHILE, I SWEAR.
I TRY TO BE A MAN OF REASON. COMPASSION. IN SHORT, YOUR OPPOSITE.

AND I ADMIT TO SCIENTIFIC CURIOSITY. HOW DID YOU DO IT, DAD? CONVINCE THEM, I MEAN.
GOOD BEHAVIOR? SAYING WHAT THEY WANTED TO HEAR?
I HAVE CHANGED, BRUCE. YOU DON'T UNDER-STAND, I...
THE THINGS I... I REMEMBERED IN THERAPY. FROM MY OWN PAST, THAT I BURIED...

TERRIBLE THINGS MY OWN FATHER DID TO ME, THE... THE...
...
I HAD... NO IDEA.

REMEMBER HOW YOU USED TO TURN ONLY AT NIGHT, BRUCE?

SMALL WONDER.

THE NIGHT... IT BRINGS OUT THE WORST IN US.

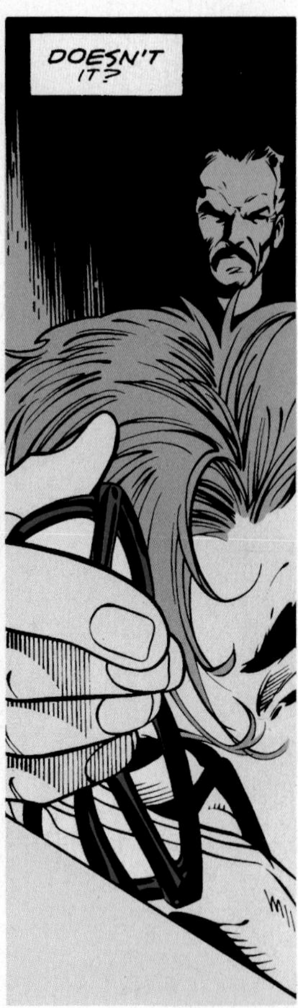
DOESN'T IT?

KNOCK! KNOCK!
16

KNOCK! KNOCK!

KNOCK! KNOCK!
WHAT WERE YOU DOING WITH THAT KNIFE, FATHER?
THERE'S SOMEONE AT THE DOOR.
THE KNIFE, DAD. WHY?

I HEARD SOMEONE *POUNDING* AWAY. I WANTED TO ***PROTECT*** MYSELF.

DSU

GENERAL ROSS. WHAT ARE YOU ***DOING*** HERE?

YOU HAVEN'T BEEN IN TOUCH SINCE WE MET LAST WEEK, BANNER. SO I DECIDED TO FOLLOW IT UP.

16

AND ***YOU*** ARE --?

BRUCE'S FATHER BRIAN. IT'S AN ***HONOR,*** GENERAL. I'M A VETERAN ***MYSELF.***

16

YOU'RE A ***MURDERER,*** SIR. GET OUT OF MY SIGHT.

YOUR GENERATION LOVES TO CALL "MILITARY INTELLIGENCE" AN OXYMORON, BUT THE FACT IS, WE HAVE AN EXTENSIVE DOSSIER ON YOU, BANNER. A DOSSIER I'VE MEMORIZED.
HOW CAN YOU LET THAT... THING ...NEAR YOU?
HE'S MY FATHER. THE DOCTORS SAY HE'S CHANGED. HE...

I'M NOT SURE I WANT TO WORK WITH YOU NOW, BANNER. YOU PRESENTED YOURSELF AS A MAN OF CONSCIENCE. I COULD ALMOST RESPECT THAT.
NOW YOU JUST SEEM LIKE A SPINELESS MILKSOP.

I RESENT THAT, GENERAL, AND FRANKLY, IT'S NONE OF YOUR BUSINESS! HE'S MY FATHER--!

AND WHEN YOU'RE AROUND HIM, YOU REVERT TO INFANCY.
BE A MAN, BANNER. IF NOT FOR YOUR LATE MOTHER'S SAKE, THEN YOURS.
BE A MAN.
16

THIS DIDN'T HAPPEN! NONE OF IT HAPPENED!
SURE IT DID, HULK! TELL ME-- WHY WOULD A MAN WHO "DESPISED" VIOLENCE... CREATE A WEAPON OF VIOLENCE?
YOU SHUT OUT WHAT ALTERED YOUR MINDSET.

YOU'VE BEEN SHOUTING FOR "MORE," MISSING THE BRUCE BANNER PART OF YOU... BUT YOU'VE ALWAYS DISDAINED BANNER.
MAYBE YOU SENSE THAT HE HELPED PROTECT YOU FROM THINGS YOU'D RATHER NOT FACE.

TELL ME, HULK... HOW DID BRIAN BANNER DIE?
THE ANNIVERSARY... OF HER DEATH...

...THERE WERE SOME MUGGERS... OR HE FELL, I THINK...
...HE WALKED AWAY, AND...

NO.
EVERY TIME YOU THINK YOU'VE MADE PEACE WITH BRIAN... HE HAUNTS YOU AGAIN.

DON'T YOU WONDER WHY? IS THERE SOME-THING THAT'S NAGGING AT YOU... SOMETHING YOU--
NO! NO!

NO, FATHER! I WANT TO BE ALONE AWHILE! YOU'VE BEEN ACTING STRANGER AND STRANGER THE PAST FEW DAYS.
PERHAPS YOU SHOULD CHECK YOURSELF BACK INTO THE--
YOU WANT TO STICK ME IN THAT PLACE AGAIN. LOCK ME AWAY FOREVER.
IT WOULD BE VOLUNTARY IF YOU CHECKED YOURSELF IN. YOU COULD LEAVE AS YOU PLEASE.

MY FIRST CONCERN IS YOU. THINGS ARE EATING AWAY AT YOU THAT POISONED YOU. POISONED YOUR RELATIONSHIPS.
YOU'RE HAVING TROUBLE DEALING WITH THEM IN THE HARSH LIGHT OF THE OUTSIDE WORLD, AND MAYBE--

MAYBE YOU'RE WHAT'S BEEN EATING AWAY AT ME! MAYBE THE REASON I GOT BETTER IN THE ASYLUM WAS BECAUSE I WAS AWAY FROM YOU!

DID YOU EVER CONSIDER THAT? MAYBE IT'S NOT IN ME!
MAYBE IT'S IN YOU! AND MAYBE THE FACT THAT I SEE THROUGH YOU SCARES THE SPIT OUT OF YOU!
I DON'T HAVE TO LISTEN TO THIS.
GET BACK HERE!

IT ALL WENT DOWN AT THE GRAVE-YARD, DIDN'T IT, BRUCE?
SO... YOU ARE HERE.

WHERE ELSE SHOULD I BE, "FATHER"...
...OTHER THAN BY MY MOTHER'S SIDE ON THE ANNIVERSARY OF HER MURDER.

YOU'VE GOT SOME NERVE COMING HERE TODAY!
BACK OFF, MONSTER!
REBECCA
BANNE
REST
PE

MONSTER? YOU STILL SUFFER THAT DELUSION?!

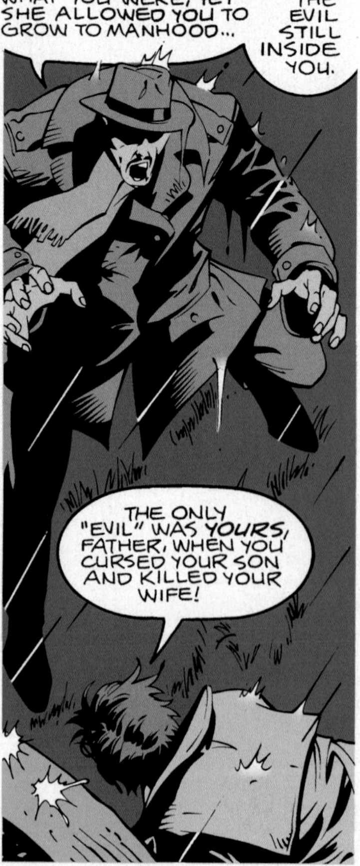
YOUR MOTHER WAS A FOOL! SHE KNEW WHAT YOU WERE, YET SHE ALLOWED YOU TO GROW TO MANHOOD...
...WITH THE EVIL STILL INSIDE YOU.
THE ONLY "EVIL" WAS YOURS, FATHER, WHEN YOU CURSED YOUR SON AND KILLED YOUR WIFE!

NO! WHAT I'VE DONE... WHAT I'M ABOUT TO DO ...WILL BE DONE FOR THE SAKE OF MANKIND!

IT ALL BOILED OVER, DIDN'T IT, BRUCE? THE RAGE, THE ANGER.

VIOLENCE HAD NEVER BEEN THE ANSWER, BUT HERE HE WAS COMING AT YOU AGAIN.
REBECCA BANNER REST IN PEACE

YOUR MIND CRIED OUT FOR PROTECTION. YOUR MOTHER CRIED OUT FOR VENGEANCE.
AND YOU LASHED OUT AT HIM, DRIVEN BY PENT-UP FURY, FRUSTRATION, AND NOT A LITTLE FEAR.

REBECCA
WAM!

REBECCA BANNER

YOU DIDN'T STOP SCREAMING FOR A VERY LONG WHILE. AND WHAT WAS ODD WAS...
...YOU KEPT YELLING "NO" WHILE, AT THE SAME TIME...
...YOUR VOICE WAS CHOKED WITH LAUGHTER.

NOOOOOO
KIRBY

THEY FOUND HIM THE NEXT DAY, WHEN YOU REPORTED HIM MISSING. RAIN WASHED AWAY ALL THE FOOTPRINTS, AND THE COPS--WHO NEVER LIKED HIM--HAPPILY WROTE IT OFF AS A RANDOM MUGGING.
MAYBE THE REASON YOU CARRY YOUR FEAR OF YOUR DAD WITH YOU ...IS THAT YOU'RE AFRAID HE'LL COME FOR YOU.
HECK, YOU EVEN DEVELOPED THE ABILITY TO SEE GHOSTS--LIKE DOC STRANGE'S ASTRAL FORM--JUST SO YOU COULD WATCH OUT FOR HIM.

MAYBE YOUR VERY CREATION WAS JUST THE BEGINNING OF HIS PUNISHMENT FROM BEYOND THE GRAVE. AND MAYBE HE WILL COME AFTER YOU SOME DAY ...TO FINISH THE JOB.
COME ALONG, PEOPLE. I'VE GOT THIS FUNNY FEELING THAT... MORE THAN EVER...
KIRBY THEATER

"HULK JUST WANTS TO BE LEFT ALONE."

I KNEW THERE WAS A DEATH AND A GRAVEYARD SOMEWHERE IN THERE.
AS FOR WHO DIED... AND WHO WAS BURIED...

...WELL, WE'RE ALL GUILTY OF FORGETTING THE LITTLE DETAILS SOMETIMES.
AREN'T WE, DOCTOR BANNER?

I...I'M DEAD.
THE MONSTER KILLED ME...
AND SENT YOU TO HELL.

AND WHEN YOU TRIED TO FIGHT BACK? GET A LITTLE JUSTICE FROM YOUR LOWLY POSITION?
HE SENT YOU LOWER STILL.

WHO ARE YOU...?

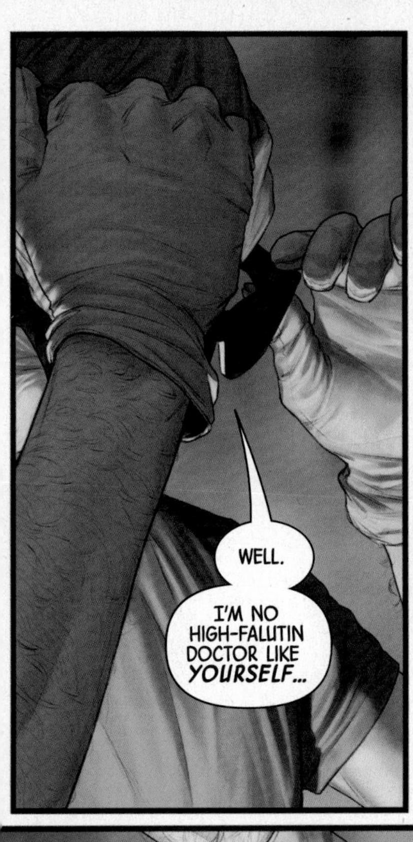
WELL.
I'M NO HIGH-FALUTIN DOCTOR LIKE YOURSELF...

BUT EVEN AS A HIGH SCHOOL DROPOUT-- I HAD AMBITION.
I KNEW ONE DAY I'D MAKE A NAME FOR MYSELF...

...EVEN IF I COULDN'T MAKE IT AS SAM STERNS.
TAKE MY HAND, DOCTOR.

OH, WAIT... YOU ALREADY DID.
REMEMBER?
NO...
YOU TOOK MY HAND. AND NOW WE ARE ONE.
THIS IS WHERE YOU LIVE NOW, BRIAN.
NO!
NO!

WELCOME HOME!
WELCOME HOME!
WELCOME HOME!
FATHER?
IS THAT *YOU...?*
WHO ELSE WOULD IT BE?

AT GROUND ZERO

AL EWING WRITER **MATTIA DE IULIS** ARTIST; COVER ARTIST **VC'S CORY PETIT** LETTERER

SARAH BRUNSTAD ASSOCIATE EDITOR **WIL MOSS** EDITOR **TOM BREVOORT** EXECUTIVE EDITOR **C.B. CEBULSKI** EDITOR IN CHIEF

JOE BENNETT
+
RUY JOSÉ MOUNTS

THEN.

I WAS NEVER AFRAID TO DIE.

AND THEN I *DIED.*

I REMEMBER A FIRECRACKER SOUND.
A HARD PUNCH TO MY BACK.
A FEELING OF SOMETHING GONE HORRIBLY WRONG.
EVERYTHING FLIPPED AND SPUN. REVERSED ITSELF.

MY COUSIN'S VOICE--BUT STRANGE. GUTTURAL.
HANG IN THERE, KID! YER GONNA MAKE IT!
A VOICE OF GRAY STONE.
YA GOTTA MAKE IT!
A BURNING SENSATION IN MY ARM.
A SENSATION LIKE FALLING. DOWN AND DOWN, FOREVER AND EVER...

DOWN BELOW.
YOU BEAR MY MARK
BUT I'D BEEN SHOT. I WAS DYING.
IT'S NO SURPRISE IF I REMEMBER SOME STRANGE SENSATIONS.

IT PROBABLY
DOESN'T MEAN
ANYTHING.

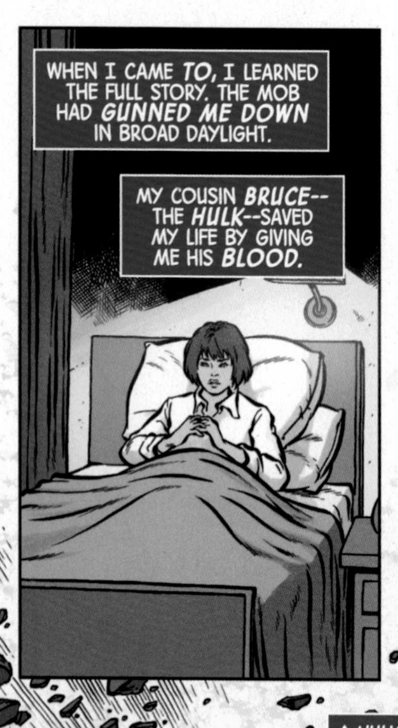

WHEN I CAME *TO*, I LEARNED THE FULL STORY. THE MOB HAD *GUNNED ME DOWN* IN BROAD DAYLIGHT.
MY COUSIN *BRUCE*-- THE *HULK*--SAVED MY LIFE BY GIVING ME HIS *BLOOD.*

SAVED IT...
...AND *CHANGED* IT.

I WAS REBORN AS SOMETHING *NEW.*

A HULK. BUT *BETTER.*

I WAS *ANGRY*-- GETTING SHOT WILL *DO* THAT--BUT FROM THE START, I HAD IT UNDER *CONTROL.*

THAT WAS *THEN.*

THIS IS NOW.

NOW.

HULK SMASH!

TANTRUM IS SOMEONE I TANGLED WITH A WHILE BACK. AS BAD GUYS GO, HE ISN'T COMPLICATED.

HE LIKES ROBBERY--WITH PLENTY OF EXTRA CHAOS SO HE CAN FEED ON THE FEAR HE CREATES. HIS MUTANT POWER TURNS THAT INTO STRENGTH.

THE COTATI INVASION LEFT PEOPLE TERRIFIED.

IT MUST HAVE BEEN LIKE AN OPEN BUFFET...

HA! YOU'RE ANGRY, AREN'T YOU, SHE-HULK? I CAN TASTE IT!

AND IT JUST MAKES ME STRONGER--

FINE BY ME. LET'S PUT ON A SHOW, SHE-HUL--
SNIKT
AND THAT'S THAT.
DIDN'T LOOK LIKE THE BRUTE FORCE APPROACH WAS WORKIN'. FIGURED I'D SNEAK UP AND CUT IT SHORT.
HOPE YOU DON'T MIND.
HULK NOT MIND, WOLVERINE... BUT...
YOU...KILL TANTRUM...?
SNAKT
WE GOT... HEALERS ON KRAKOA. SPECIAL ONES.
TRUST ME.
HE'LL LIVE.

HE'S GONNA FACE OUR JUSTICE. PRETTY SURE HE BROKE MUTANT LAW BACK THERE.
BUT TECHNICALLY... HE'S GOT A PLACE ON THE ISLAND LIKE ANYONE ELSE.

ANYONE ELSE WHO'S MUTANT, ANYWAY.
HRH.
NICE FOR SOME.

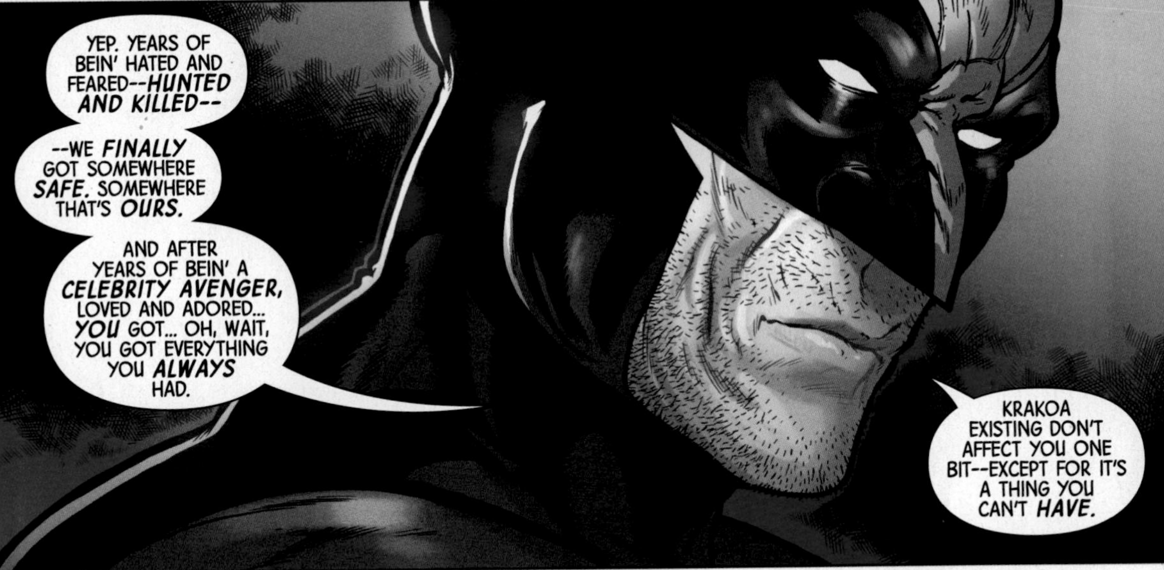
YEP. YEARS OF BEIN' HATED AND FEARED--HUNTED AND KILLED--
--WE FINALLY GOT SOMEWHERE SAFE, SOMEWHERE THAT'S OURS.
AND AFTER YEARS OF BEIN' A CELEBRITY AVENGER, LOVED AND ADORED... YOU GOT... OH, WAIT, YOU GOT EVERYTHING YOU ALWAYS HAD.
KRAKOA EXISTING DON'T AFFECT YOU ONE BIT--EXCEPT FOR IT'S A THING YOU CAN'T HAVE.

NICE FOR SOME.

HULK... WANT TALK, LOGAN.
NEED QUIET, THOUGH... AND...

...AND I THINK I NEED PROPER SENTENCES.
CAN WE GO SOMEWHERE AND GET A BEER?

...WELL, THIS IS QUIET, ALL RIGHT.
TOOK THIS BAR A WHILE TO GET BACK ON ITS FEET AFTER EVERYTHING. THEY JUST FINISHED RESTOCKING--PLACE OPENS IN A COUPLE DAYS.
THE OWNER'S AN OLD FRIEND FROM BACK IN THE DAY--SHE GAVE ME A SET OF KEYS.
I WATCHED YOU PICK THE LOCK WITH A CLAW.
I DIDN'T SAY I HAD 'EM ON ME.
WHAT DID YOU WANNA TALK ABOUT?
'CAUSE IF IT'S A HULKS-GOT-IT-WORSE SPEECH, I HEARD IT A FEW TIMES ALREADY...
WHAT WAS IT LIKE? FOR YOU, I MEAN.
WHAT WAS WHAT LIKE?
COMING BACK FROM THE DEAD.
...
THAT'S A BIG QUESTION, WALTERS.

BIGGER THAN YOU THINK IT IS.
THERE'S... STUFF IT AIN'T A GOOD IDEA FOR ME TO *TALK* ABOUT, OKAY?

WHAT, *FORBIDDEN KNOWLEDGE* FROM *BEYOND THE VEIL?*
STUFF I DON'T WANNA TELL YOU.
STUFF YOU DON'T WANNA *KNOW.*

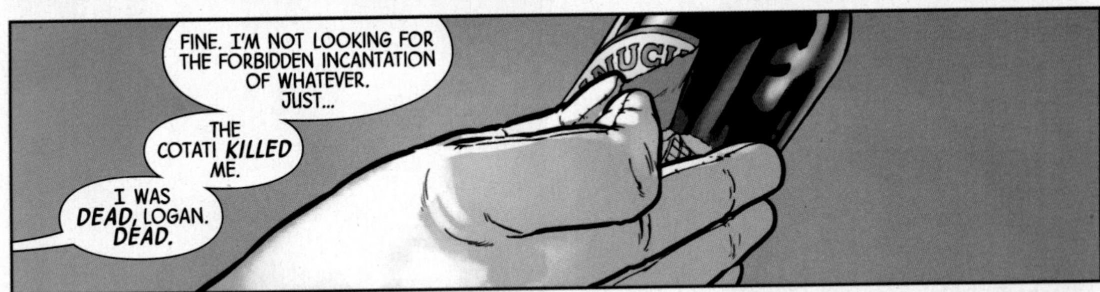
FINE. I'M NOT LOOKING FOR THE FORBIDDEN INCANTATION OF WHATEVER. JUST...
THE COTATI *KILLED* ME.
I WAS *DEAD,* LOGAN. *DEAD.*

AND NOW I'M *NOT.*
AND IT'S NOT THE *FIRST TIME* EITHER. IT MIGHT BE THE *THIRD* TIME. THERE MIGHT BE A *FOURTH.*

YOU'VE BEEN DEAD. YOU'VE BEEN BURIED IN *ADAMANTIUM,* BLOWN UP BY A *NUKE*...AND YEAH, SURE, *"HEALING FACTOR,"* BUT...
PALE ALE

BUT YOU'VE BEEN *THROUGH* THIS.
HOW DO I DEAL WITH IT?

...
ARE YOU STILL THE SAME YOU?

...SURE. I MEAN, IT'S THE SAME BODY, I'M THE SAME PERSON...
SO STOP LOOKIN' IT IN THE MOUTH.

WHAT?
LOOK-- YOU COME BACK FROM STUFF THAT SHOULDA KILLED YOU. THAT DID KILL YOU.
AND I WON'T LIE--FIRST TIME, SECOND TIME, THAT'LL SHAKE YOU UP.

BUT IT'S YOU. YOUR FRIENDS-- THEY SEE YOU. THEY KNOW YOU. IT'S YOU.
SO... YEAH.
"HEALING FACTOR."

SAME AS YER COUSIN, SAME AS...A LOT OF PEOPLE THESE DAYS...
YOU HEAL FROM WORSE STUFF THAN MOST, BUT IT'S STILL JUST HEALING. ALL IT NEEDS TO BE.

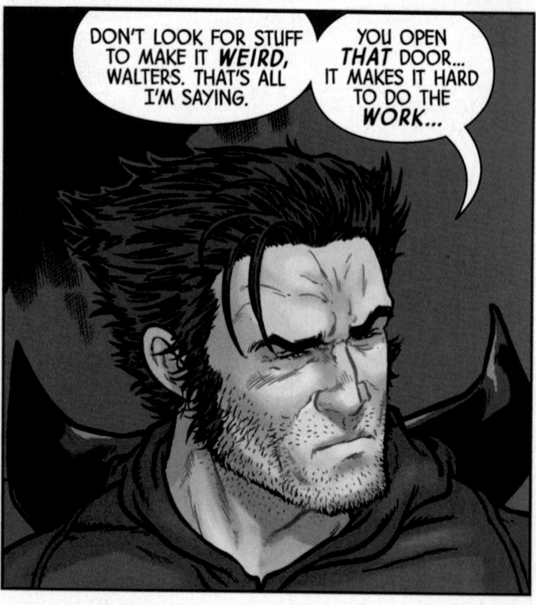
DON'T LOOK FOR STUFF TO MAKE IT WEIRD, WALTERS. THAT'S ALL I'M SAYING.
YOU OPEN THAT DOOR... IT MAKES IT HARD TO DO THE WORK...

THEN.
"...AND THE WORK ALWAYS NEEDS DOIN'."
ON THAT, I AGREE WITH LOGAN. THE WORK ALWAYS NEEDS DOING.

THIS WAS... WHEN? A YEAR AGO? TWO?
THERE WAS A GUY WHO COULD SEE THE FUTURE.
HE GAVE US THREE HOURS' WARNING THAT THANOS WAS ABOUT TO STEAL A COSMIC CUBE AND KILL THE WORLD WITH IT.
THREE HOURS ISN'T LONG.

WE PUT TOGETHER EVERYONE WE COULD FIND. SOME OF THE HEAVIEST HITTERS ON THIS PLANET.

BUT IT WASN'T ENOUGH--NOT TO DO IT *CLEAN.*

PEOPLE DIED. *JIM RHODES* DIED.

I DIED.

BUT NOT RIGHT AWAY.

I REMEMBER TONY STARK JUST... SHRIEKING AT CAROL DANVERS. AT MY HOSPITAL BEDSIDE, NO LESS.
WE'D PAID IN BLOOD TO SAVE THE WORLD, BUT TONY HADN'T BEEN CONSULTED, SO IT DIDN'T COUNT.

HE WAS LITERALLY ARGUING THAT WE SHOULDN'T HAVE HAD THE WARNING.
I TELL MYSELF NOW IT WAS HIS GRIEF TALKING. I HAVE TO--I WORK WITH HIM.

BUT THE TRUTH IS, IF I'D BEEN ON MY FEET, I'D HAVE BROKEN HIS JAW.
FIGHT FOR IT.
WE'D LOST SO MUCH TO SAVE SO MANY LIVES, AND HE DIDN'T CARE. I WAS SO ANGRY...

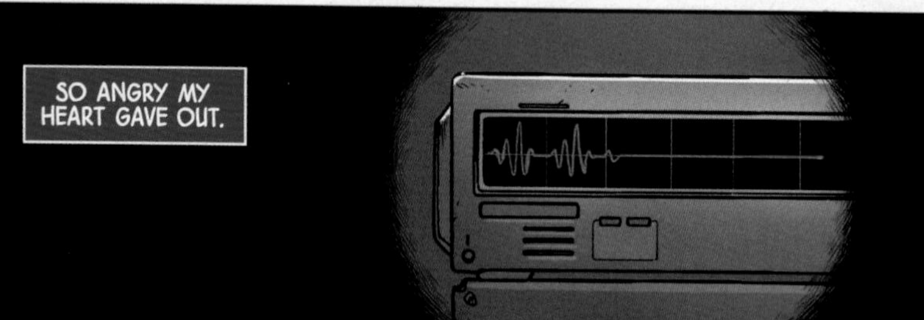

SO ANGRY MY HEART GAVE OUT.
TO BE FAIR, THERE WAS STILL SHRAPNEL IN IT FROM A THANOS-KILLING MISSILE.

I FLATLINED. THEY DIDN'T KNOW HOW TO REVIVE ME. THAT WAS THAT.

YOU COULD SAY TONY STARK'S NEED TO ALWAYS BE RIGHT GOT ME KILLED.

AND NOT EVEN FOR THE LAST TIME.

I DON'T KNOW WHAT HAPPENED NEXT.
... GOOD GOD.
JENNIFER? ELLIE'S DAUGHTER? WHAT ARE YOU DOING HERE...?
DON'T YOU RECOGNIZE ME? YOU AND MY SON WERE SO CLOSE...
IT'S ME, JEN.
IT'S YOUR UNCLE BRIAN.
"THERE'S SOMETHING I NEED TO TELL YOU, HONEY."

YOUR... YOUR AUNT REBECCA WAS KILLED YESTERDAY.
SHE AND YOUR UNCLE BRIAN...THEY HAD A FIGHT, AND...
...HE SAYS THERE WAS AN ACCIDENT.
...
IS THAT TRUE?
SHERIFF
UNCLE BRIAN.
I'M IN *HELL*, AREN'T I?
I DIED AND WENT TO HELL.

HA! NO, NO. IT'S MUCH WORSE THAN THAT.
I WAS ALREADY IN HELL, YOU SEE.

I DID TRY TO ESCAPE IT, WHEN THE OPPORTUNITY CAME. RETURN TO THE LAND OF THE LIVING.
DEFEAT THE MONSTER, THE SICKNESS LIVING IN MY SON...

...THE DEVIL THAT SMASHED MY HEAD OPEN ON MY WIFE'S OWN GRAVE.
AFTER EVERYTHING I DID FOR THEM.

YOU MURDERED YOUR WIFE AND DESTROYED YOUR SON. YOU MADE YOUR OWN PLACE IN HELL, UNCLE BRIAN.
AND YOUR "ESCAPE" WAS COMING BACK AS A GIANT SCALY MONSTER. I WAS THERE.
REMEMBER?
"REMEMBER HOW HARD MY FAMILY TOOK YOU DOWN?"

"TOOK ME DOWN." VERY APPROPRIATE CHOICE OF WORDS, YOUNG LADY.
YOU DID INDEED TAKE ME ALL THE WAY DOWN... PAST THE COUNTRY OF HELL...

...TO WHAT LIES BELOW IT.
HELL ACTUALLY SEEMS QUAINT TO ME NOW. IT HAD HIERARCHIES AND STRUCTURES. RULERS AND RULES.
IT WAS ONLY A PLACE, LIKE OTHER PLACES...

...AND THIS IS SOMETHING ELSE. SOMETHING DEEPER, AT THE BOTTOM OF REALITY, UNDERNEATH EVERYTHING...
THE CONCEPT OF HELL. THE FOUNDATION. THE BEDROCK.
THE BELOW-PLACE.

WE ARE SPECIAL TO IT, JENNIFER. TOUCHED BY ITS ESSENCE...ITS CONTAGION.
WE BEAR ITS MARK.

AND NOW WE'RE STUCK HERE? FOREVER? IS THAT IT?
I GOT THE WRONG KIND OF RADIATION AND NOW I'M TRAPPED FOREVER IN HELL? HOW DOES THAT MAKE SENSE?
YOU'RE NOT.

WHAT...?
THERE WAS SOMEONE ELSE HERE WITH ME BEFORE. LEONARD SAMSON-- A DEAD PSYCHIATRIST. A QUACK.
HE KEPT... TALKING AT ME... TELLING ME WHAT WAS WRONG WITH ME, AS IF HE COULD KNOW...
BUT THEN HE LEFT. BACK TO LIFE.
THROUGH A GREEN DOOR.
YOU WILL TOO.
THE DOOR DOESN'T OPEN FOR ME--NOT TO LET ME THROUGH. BUT ALL THE SAME...
I'M LEARNING HOW TO LOOK THROUGH IT.
I'M LEARNING SO MUCH...
I DON'T REMEMBER WHAT HAPPENED AFTER I DIED.
BUT THAT WASN'T THE PROBLEM.

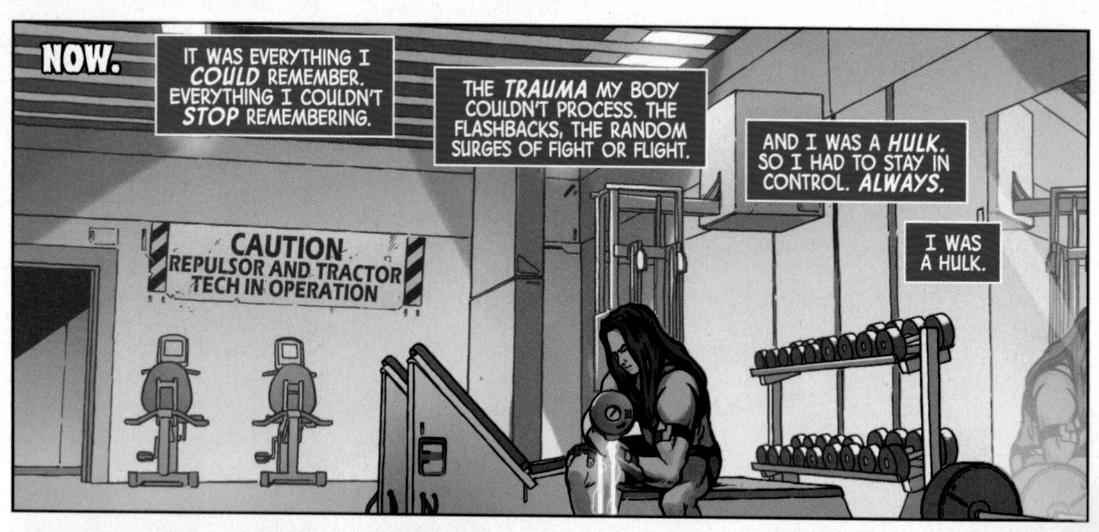

NOW.
IT WAS EVERYTHING I COULD REMEMBER. EVERYTHING I COULDN'T STOP REMEMBERING.
THE TRAUMA MY BODY COULDN'T PROCESS. THE FLASHBACKS, THE RANDOM SURGES OF FIGHT OR FLIGHT.
AND I WAS A HULK. SO I HAD TO STAY IN CONTROL. ALWAYS.
I WAS A HULK.
CAUTION
REPULSOR AND TRACTOR
TECH IN OPERATION

SO EVERYONE COULD SEE.
I FELT BROKEN. TAINTED.
SOMETIMES I STILL DO.

I KEEP IT TO MYSELF.

THOR?

WANT... TRAIN WITH HULK?

...

AYE, WHY NOT?

NEW COSTUME LOOKS GOOD ON THOR.
HULK LIKED BEARD, THOUGH...
AS DID I-- BEFORE I WAS ALL-FATHER.

BUT IT BEGAN TO FEEL LIKE MY FATHER WAS GAZING AT ME FROM THE MIRROR...
HRH. YES.
IMPORTANT TO LOOK IN MIRROR.

THE THRONE OF ASGARD IS...NOT A COMFORTABLE ONE. PERHAPS SOMEDAY I WILL GROW MORE USED TO IT.
THOR HAS FOREVER. FOREVER IS A LOT OF SOMEDAYS.
LOT OF TIME TO CHANGE...

I SUPPOSE IT MUST SEEM THAT WAY TO MORTALS.
OFTTIMES, I FIND MYSELF SHAMED BY HOW LITTLE CHANGING WE GODS SEEM TO--
HULK NOT MORTAL.

...WHAT?
HULK NOT MORTAL, THOR.

HULK NOT DIE.

OR...HULK DIES, BUT HULK COMES BACK. HULK IS A HULK. AN IMMORTAL HULK.
HULK HAS FOREVER, LIKE THOR...BUT ONLY STARTING.
WHAT FOREVER LIKE FROM OTHER END?
...
A VAST QUESTION.
WOULD YOU RATHER TALK ABOUT IT AS JENNIFER?
TRIED. FELT... TOO HEAVY FOR JEN.
NEEDS HULK TO BEAR IT.
WELL...I AM SORRY, HULK.
BUT IT WILL GROW HEAVIER.
AS YOU SAY--YOU ARE AT THE START, AND SO YOU CANNOT SEE THE FINISH.
BUT WHETHER MY FINISH IS MILLENNIA HENCE OR...SOONER THAN I WOULD LIKE...IT IS STILL WRITTEN.
"I REMEMBER GALACTUS.
"HE WAS IMMORTAL BY ANY MEASURE. HE SURVIVED THE DEATH OF A MULTIVERSE, THE BIRTH OF ANOTHER, AND LIVED MILLENNIA BEYOND THAT.
"AND STILL, I LOOKED HIM IN THE EYE...

"...AND I BROUGHT THAT TO AN END."

THOR...KILLED GALACTUS...?
IT FELT LIKE JUSTICE, AT THE TIME.*
IN ANY CASE, THE DEED IS DONE.
*SEE THOR (2020) #6. -WIL

HE WAS IMMORTAL, AND NOW HE IS DEAD.
AS WILL I BE, AS WILL YOU.
THAT IS ALL THE ADVICE I HAVE, HULK.

TO REMEMBER...
...THAT THERE ARE NONE WHO HAVE FOREVER.

OH, I REMEMBER.

THEN.
I REMEMBER THE THIRD TIME I DIED.
I WAS ON THE MOON, MAKING FRIENDS WITH THE COTATI.
THE SAME COTATI WHO INVADED EARTH, WHO WANTED TO WIPE OUT THE GALAXY...BUT TONY THOUGHT THEY WERE THE GOOD GUYS. AND TONY ALWAYS HAS TO BE RIGHT.
NOT THAT I KNEW BETTER. I'D LIKE TO SAY I SUSPECTED--BUT THAT WOULD BE A LIE.
I'M NOT STUPID WHEN I'M HULK.
WORDS ARE HARDER FOR ME--FRAGILE SHELLS FOR MY BLAZING GREEN THOUGHTS.
HULK?
HRH?
THAT DOESN'T MAKE ME STUPID.
FOLLOW ME. YOU'LL NEED A WEAPON AGAINST THE ENEMY.
HULK NOT NEED PUNY SWORD--
BUT I WAS STUPID THEN.
TRUST ME.
YOU'LL NEED THIS.

THEY SPLIT ME OFF FROM THE OTHERS. TRUSTING AS A LAMB.
I HAD A SECOND TO FEEL THE TENDRILS TAKE MY LEGS OUT FROM UNDER ME--

THEN THEY WERE TEARING INTO MY BRAIN.
YOU'RE SURE THEY'RE STRONG ENOUGH? SHE'S A HULK...

THESE TENDRILS ARE CENTAURIAN IRONWOOD, SWORDSMAN.
STRONGER THAN A BATTLESHIP'S HULL...

...AND BLESSED BY OUR MESSIAH.
YOU MUST HAVE MORE FAITH...
YES...YES, FAITH...

FAITH.

THEY MURDERED ME JUST TO HIDE IN MY CORPSE. WORE IT LIKE A SUIT OF CLOTHES TO INFILTRATE THE AVENGERS.

SO I'M TOLD, ANYWAY.

I WASN'T THERE.
GOOD LORD. IS THAT JENNIFER WALTERS?
IT'S BEEN A DOG'S AGE.

HOLY CRAP.
SAM STERNS? THE LEADER? IS THAT YOU?
WHAT IS THIS-- SOME POCKET DIMENSION YOU MADE? ARE YOU IN LEAGUE WITH THE COTATI?

IT FEELS FAMILIAR... BUT...
YOU REMEMBER PREVIOUS VISITS? TELL ME MORE.
THIS IS INVALUABLE DATA...

I DO REMEMBER... THERE'S A DOOR OUT, ISN'T THERE?
A GREEN DOOR.
I'M GOING TO COME BACK TO LIFE. LIKE BRUCE, LIKE LEONARD...LIKE YOU.

YES! WONDERFUL!
THAT'S WHAT LED ME TO THE GREEN DOOR, TO THE ONE BELOW ALL... TO MY NEW PLANS.
PLANS SO VAST, SO AMBITIOUS... THEY SPAN TO THE END OF TIME.
WHICH, AS A GAMMA MUTATE, I WILL SEE...

YOU'RE FORGETTING SOMETHING, STERNS. YOU'RE NOT THE ONLY GAMMA MUTATE OUT THERE. AND THE REST OF US DON'T LIKE YOU VERY MUCH.
I GUESS WE'LL BE USING THAT BIG HEAD AS A FOOTBALL UNTIL THE END OF TIME...

OH, JEN. JEN, JEN, JEN...
YOU GUESS WRONG.

NOW.
AND THEN I CAME BACK.
AAAHHH!
THERE WASN'T TIME TO QUESTION IT. NOT THEN.
SO I BURNED THE COTATI OUT OF MY SYSTEM. I JOINED THE FINAL BATTLE.
I KICKED BUTT, I TOOK NAMES. I DID WHAT AVENGERS DO.
UHHN... NO...NO, NO, NO...
AND WHEN I FINALLY DID START QUESTIONING...
NNRRAAARGH!
WOLVERINE TOLD ME IT DIDN'T CHANGE ANYTHING. THOR TOLD ME IMMORTALITY DIDN'T EXIST.
IGNORE IT, DENY IT, FORGET IT.
AND THE WORST PART IS... MAYBE THEY'RE RIGHT. MAYBE I SHOULD DO THAT...BECAUSE SOMETHING HAPPENED LAST TIME.
I DON'T REMEMBER WHAT, BUT SOMETHING HAPPENED.

AND IT SCARED ME.
YOU WON'T BE USING MY HEAD AS A FOOTBALL, JEN.
FOR ONE THING, YOU WON'T EVEN REMEMBER THIS CONVERSATION.
AND FOR ANOTHER...YOU DON'T HAVE UNTIL THE END OF TIME.
YOU'RE NOT IMMORTAL. NEITHER IS BRUCE.
YOU JUST HAVE A KEY OTHERS DON'T. THE KEY TO A GREEN DOOR-- THE DOOR BACK FROM DEATH.
BUT THE TROUBLE WITH KEYS...
...IS THAT SOMETIMES, PEOPLE CHANGE THE LOCKS.
SEE? I DECIDE IF THE GREEN DOOR'S OPEN NOW.
I DECIDE IF IT'S CLOSED.
NOW... YOU'VE CAUGHT ME IN A GOOD MOOD. AND IF YOU STAYED HERE, YOU'D BE A COMPLICATION I DON'T NEED.
SO BACK YOU GO.
BUT IF YOU REMEMBER NOTHING ELSE... REMEMBER THIS.
DON'T DIE AGAIN, JEN.
DON'T EVER DIE AGAIN.
I WAS NEVER AFRAID TO DIE.

BUT THEN I DIED.
DON'T DIE AGAIN, JEN.
DON'T DIE AGAIN.

THE THREE DEATHS OF JENNIFER WALTERS

AL EWING WRITER JON DAVIS-HUNT ARTIST MARCIO MENYZ COLOR ARTIST
VC'S CORY PETIT LETTERER JOE BENNETT, RUY JOSÉ & PAUL MOUNTS (AFTER ALEX ROSS) COVER ARTISTS
SIMONE DI MEO; DANIEL WARREN JOHNSON & MIKE SPICER; ALEX ROSS VARIANT COVER ARTISTS
SARAH BRUNSTAD ASSOCIATE EDITOR WIL MOSS EDITOR TOM BREVOORT EXECUTIVE EDITOR C.B. CEBULSKI EDITOR IN CHIEF
HULK CREATED BY STAN LEE & JACK KIRBY

KUDER
2020

KNULL, THE PRIMORDIAL AND MALICIOUS **GOD OF THE SYMBIOTES**, HAS ARRIVED ON EARTH WITH AN ARMY OF SYMBIOTE DRAGONS. KNULL IS THE **KING IN BLACK.**

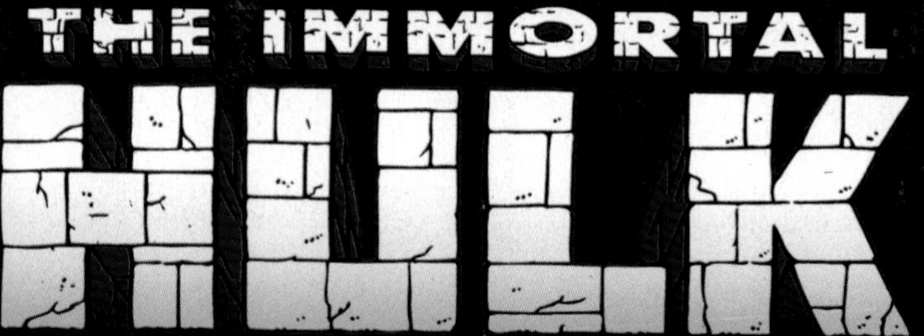

THE HULK IS IN BAD SHAPE.

DEVIL HULK, THE LOVINGLY VIOLENT PERSONA THAT HAS SOUGHT TO PROTECT BOTH HULK AND BANNER FOR DECADES, IS DEAD. AND BRUCE BANNER IS GONE — DRAGGED OUT OF HIS OWN MINDSCAPE BY THE LEADER, WHO CRACKED THE CODE TO THE HULK'S COMPLEX PERSONALITIES.

NOW ALL THAT'S LEFT IS THE CHILDLIKE SAVAGE HULK — DRAINED OF SO MUCH GAMMA THAT HE CAN BARELY WALK — AND JOE FIXIT, THE FORMER GREY HULK WHO NOW MANIFESTS IN BANNER'S BODY. SAVAGE, JOE...ANY WAY YOU CUT IT, THE HULK'S A WANTED MAN. AND HE'S IN NO SHAPE TO FACE THE DEMONIC ARMY OF A MAD GOD.

BLACK CHRISTMAS

'Twas the night before Christmas...

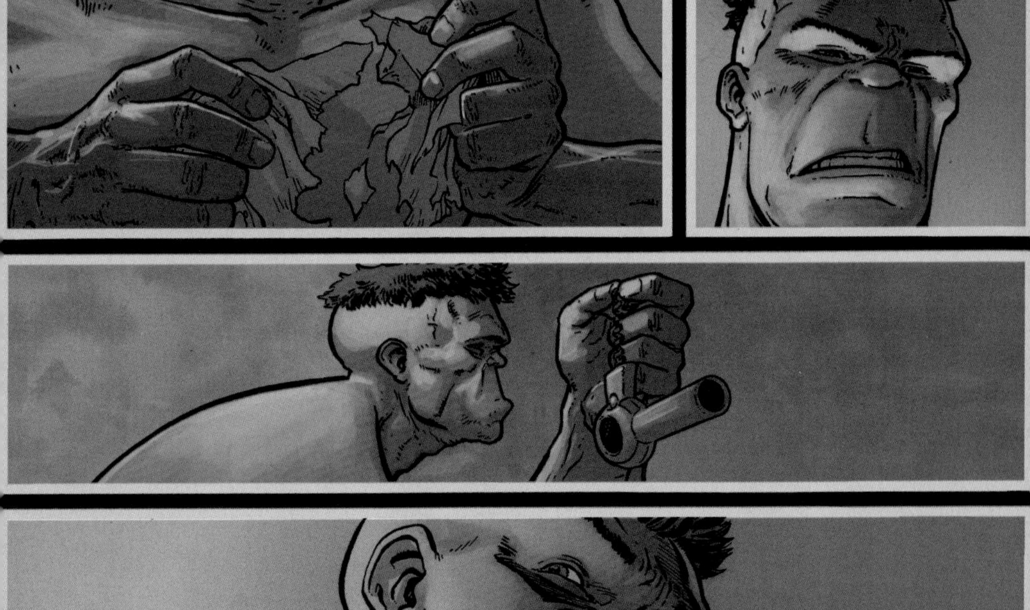

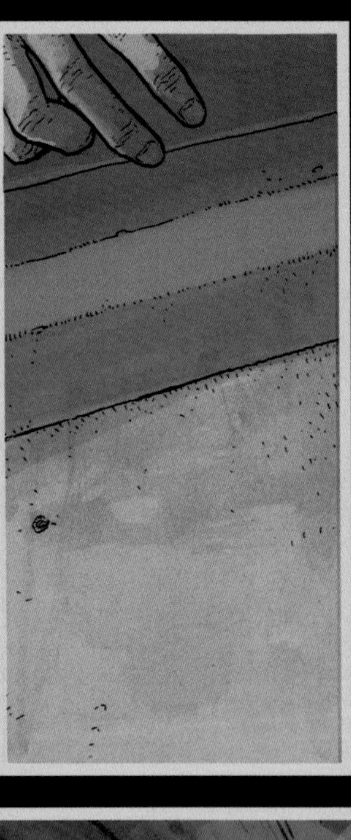

NYPD

MANTLOS

BACK
FOR
RISTMAS
MEKKANIX

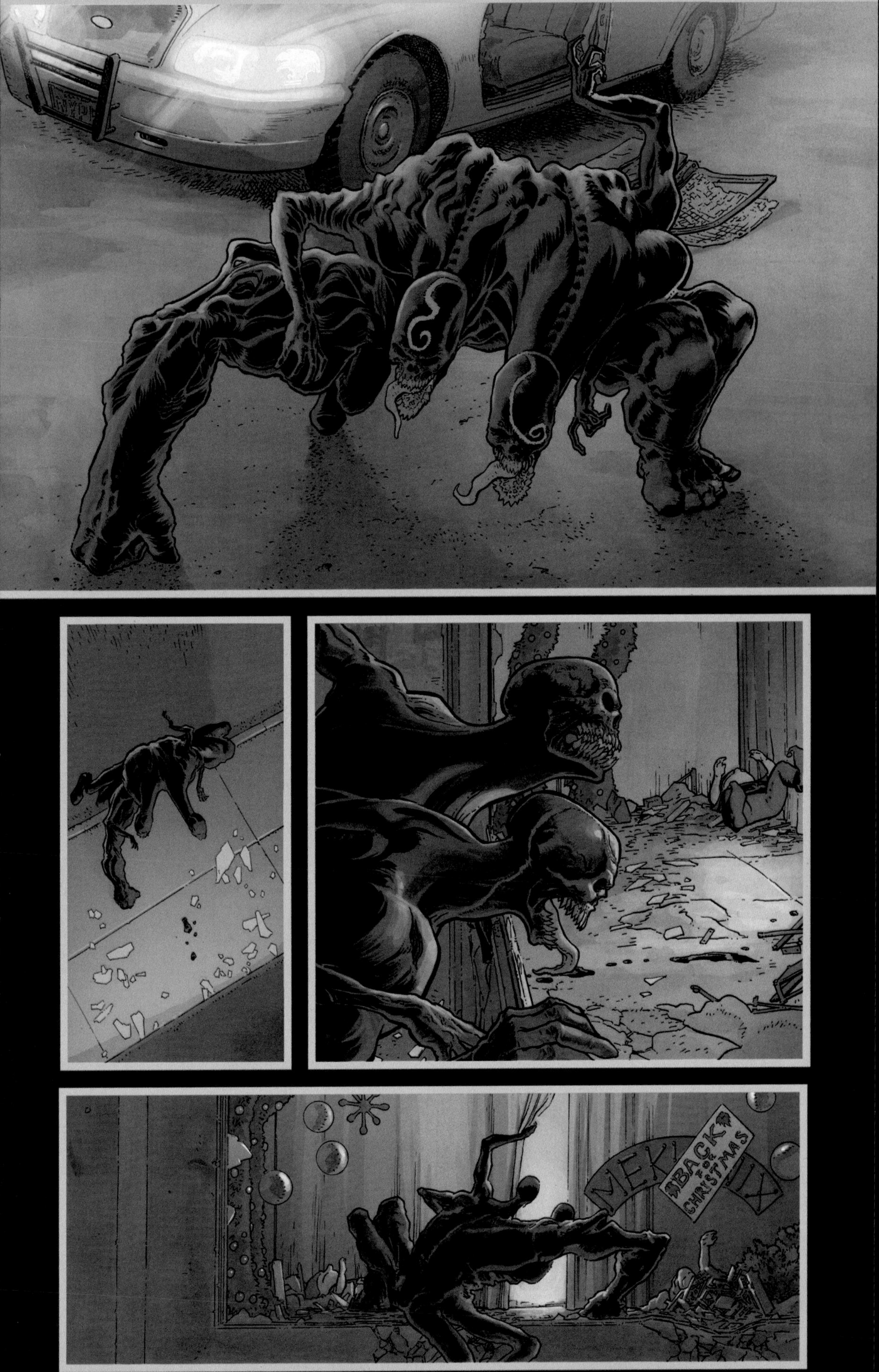

BACK FOR CHRISTMAS

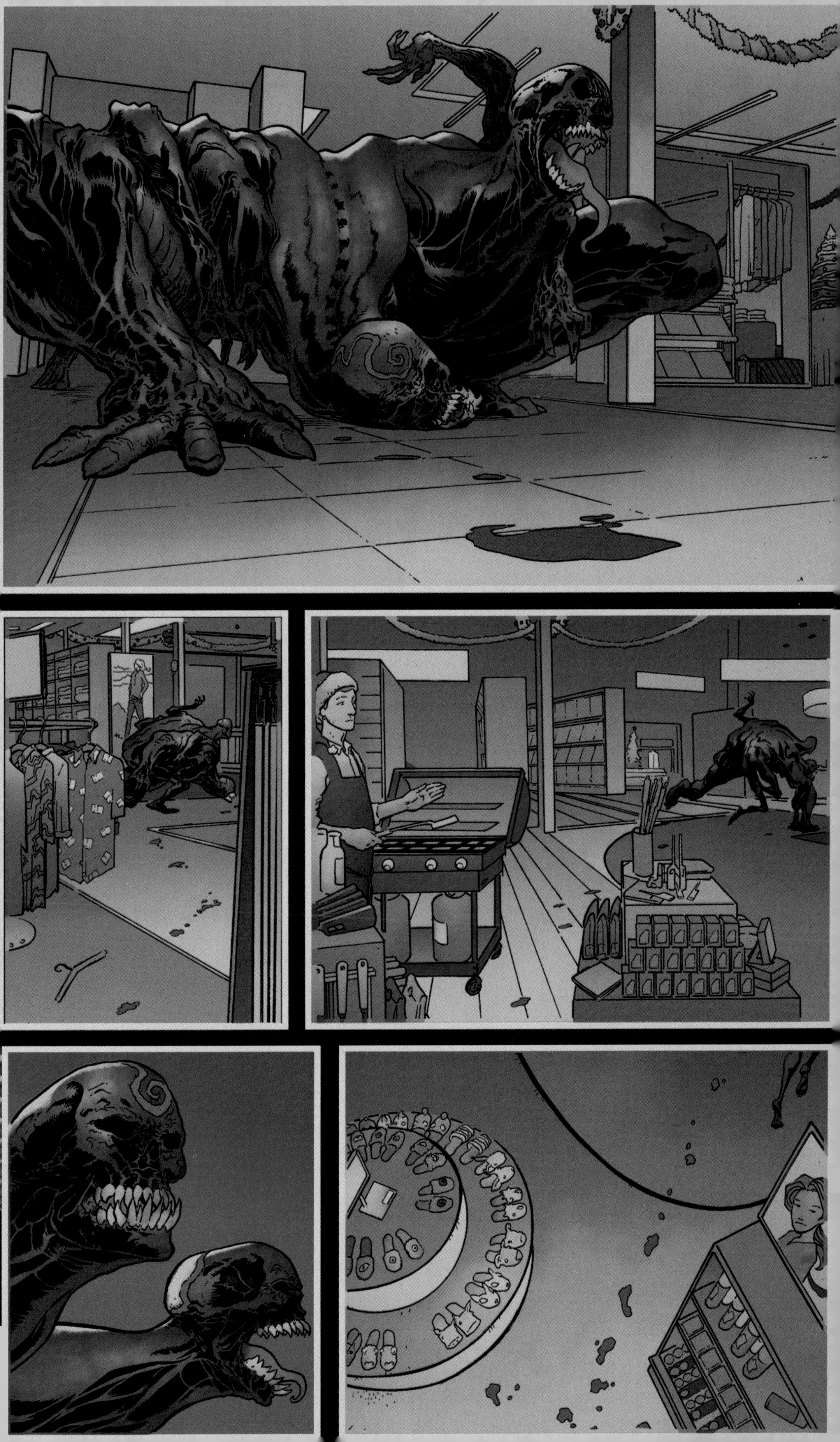

PLAY
GREG LAKE
BELIEVE IN FATHER...
2:07/ 3:32
VOL:100
KEOWN
2012 WORLD TOUR

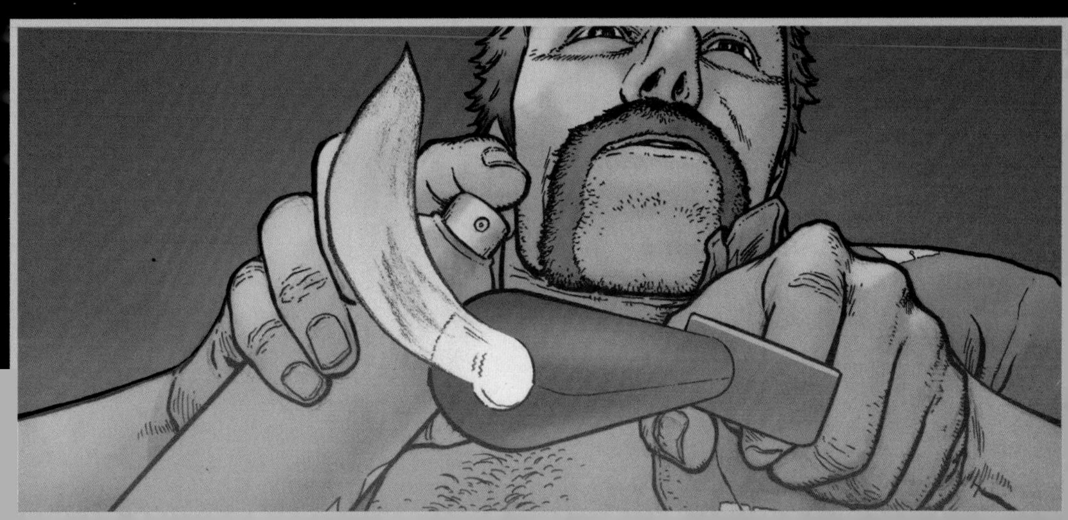

TLOS
DIRECTORY

MANTLOS

...and to all a GOOD NIGHT.

AL EWING WRITER **AARON KUDER** ARTIST
FRANK MARTIN & ERICK ARCINIEGA COLOR ARTISTS
VC'S CORY PETIT LETTERER

"IF THESE SHADOWS REMAIN UNALTERED BY THE FUTURE, THE CHILD WILL DIE."

– CHARLES DICKENS,
A CHRISTMAS CAROL

IMMORTAL HULK: TIME OF THE MONSTERS

"I BEHOLD THEE ENKIDU; LIKE A GOD THOU ART.
WHY WITH THE ANIMALS
WANDEREST THOU ON THE PLAIN?"

– *THE EPIC OF GILGAMESH*,
TRANSLATED BY STEPHEN HERBERT LANGDON

JORDAN, 9,500 BCE.
YOU'RE YOUNG, TAMMUZ. YOU WON'T REMEMBER WHEN THE MOTHER GODDESS STILL WATCHED OVER US WITH HER GOOD GREEN EYE.
WE THOUGHT IT A BLESSING AT FIRST, BUT WE WERE A PUNY PEOPLE THEN--PUNY AND PROUD. WE TOOK TALL RYE AND SWEET MILK FOR OUR BIRTHRIGHT.
BUT THE MOTHER GODDESS IS A TEACHER ABOVE ALL, SO SHE PUT OUT HER EYE AND CAST IT HERE, THE BETTER TO MARK THE SQUANDERING OF HER GIFTS.
THE GROUND SHOOK. THE SKY WAS A PILLAR OF ASH AND GREEN FLAME. WE DANCED AND WEPT FOR JOY.
BUT SOON ALL THAT FELL BENEATH THE GAZE OF THE MOTHER GODDESS' GOOD GREEN EYE BECAME ROTTED.
EVERY GRAIN. EVERY GAZELLE. EVERY PEST AND CUR.
ALL WITHERED.

YOU CAN FEEL IT HERE, CAN'T YOU...?
MAGIC SO STRONG IT STINGS THE EYES.
ADAD-- HONORED ELDER-- PLEASE.
LISTEN. SUCH MAGIC CAN BE RECKONED WITH NEITHER EASILY NOR CHEAPLY.
OUR LANDS BLACKENED LIKE A DEAD TOOTH.
KNOWING NO BETTER, OUR CHILDREN BECAME RESTLESS.
THEIR FAITH-- YOUR FAITH-- FALTERED.
MY SON LOVES YOU AS A BROTHER, TAMMUZ. HE WOULD FOLLOW YOU ANYWHERE.
THAT IS WHY I CANNOT ALLOW YOU TO LEAVE.
I KNOW WHAT YOU SAY ABOUT ME BEHIND MY BACK, BOY...
THAT MY WITS HAVE FLED. THAT I AM LEADING OUR VILLAGE TO RUIN.
BUT I KNOW WHAT THE EYE WANTS.
ALL THOSE SUMMERS OF FLASHING SICKLES AND EASY GAME.
WE TOOK... ENDLESSLY.
SOMETHING IN MY CHEST... BROKEN.
BUT WE DID NOT GIVE.

WE ARE *STARVING*, ADAD.

EVEN THE WILD HERDS HAVE ABANDONED US. THEY CAN TASTE THE *DEATH* IN OUR WATER.

WAIT... WHY ARE WE HERE?

WHY HAVE YOU BROUGHT ME BEFORE THE *EYE?*

THE ANCESTORS SPOKE TO ME.

THEY SAID THE GENTLE SEASONS WILL RETURN. IT CAN *ALL* BE PUT BACK TOGETHER.

BUT NOT WHILE THE HEAVENS ARE HALF-BLIND.

NO!

NYAARGH!!!

THERE IS NO GREAT REMEDY WITHOUT GREAT SACRIFICE, TAMMUZ!

I WILL TELL *SHALIM* YOU WERE UNAFRAID!

BUT... BUT LEAVING WASN'T...

MY IDEA.

BUT IT'S TOO LATE.

TAMMUZ FEELS THE GOOD GREEN EYE'S GAZE AND HE IS *OVERTHROWN.*

THERE'S A HISSING IN HIS EARS LIKE RAIN ON HOT STONES, AND HE WISHES IT WOULD STOP.
PRICKLING ON THE TONGUE. BUZZING IN THE BONES. A WHIRL OF NOVEL SENSATIONS.
HE WILL HAVE QUITE THE STORY TO TELL SHALIM ONCE THEY HAVE THE VILLAGE AT THEIR BACKS.
BUT PERHAPS IT IS TOO LATE TO LEAVE TODAY.
BESIDES, FIRST HE NEEDS TO BE WARM. IT IS SO VERY COLD OUT HERE WITHOUT SKINS ON ONE'S SHOULDERS.
AS HIS VISION CLOUDS, HE SEES A DOOR--A *HEAVY GREEN DOOR,* KINDLY AS A GRANDMOTHER...
...AND SOMEONE IS LOOKING THROUGH IT.

"I KNOW, MOTHER. HE'S *LATE.*"

WHEEEEEN?

WE WERE SUPPOSED TO FLEE THIS PLACE AND ITS SOUR MAGIC AT FIRST LIGHT, BUT YOU KNOW TAMMUZ; HE *DITHERS.*
PLEASE WATCH OVER HIM, MOTHER.
I HAVE A *FEELING...*
SHALIM?

WHAT DID YOU *DO* TO HIM, YOU WORM-ADDLED OLD JACKAL?!

I'VE SAVED US ALL, BOY!
KRAK!
ADAD! ADAD!
LOOK AT ME, MILKSOP!
HKKK!!!
TAMMUZ DIDN'T MAKE A SOUND WHEN THE EYE ATE OF HIS FLESH. NOT A SOUND!
HE UNDERSTOOD WHAT CIVILIZATION IS, SHALIM--WHAT IT COSTS!
HONORED ELDER--
LEAVE US!
THERE'S A BEAST IN THE GORGE! ENORMOUS! ENOUGH TO FEED US ALL FOR...
PLEASE, YOU MUST COME!
IT WORKED. THANK YOU, ANCESTORS.
COME, SHALIM. BRING YOUR BOW.

"YOU HAVE A CHANCE TO REDEEM YOURSELF YET."
TAMMUZ DOESN'T REMEMBER HOW HE GOT HERE. (WAS ADAD WITH HIM?) BUT IT HARDLY MATTERS NOW.
HE KNOWS HE SHOULD FIND SHALIM. HE KNOWS HE SHOULD STICK TO THE PLAN.
BUT HIS MIND IS DANCING WITH FOXFIRE. SO MANY IDEAS. SO MANY WAYS HE CAN HELP.
THE RAIN IS POISON, SO HE SHOULD REALLY START THERE.
STREAMS. THERE ARE STREAMS UNDERGROUND. CLEAN. PURE. WITH THE RIGHT TOOLS, THEY CAN BE TAPPED.
THE GLEAMING ROCK IS KEY. HE WILL CRUSH IT. HE WILL SMASH IT.
WITH FIRE HE WILL MELT THE GLEAM LIKE TALLOW AND SHAPE IT CUNNINGLY.
THE FIRE WILL MAKE THE TOOLS. THE TOOLS WILL MAKE THE FUTURE.

AND OF COURSE, THERE'S THE POWER. TORRENTS OF IT. ENOUGH TO BREAK WORLDS.
BUT LIKE THE STREAMS UNDERGROUND THAT FLOW WITHOUT SURCEASE, IT IS TOO CLEAN AND TOO PURE TO BE DANGEROUS.
HE WILL SHARE THIS POWER WITH HIS VILLAGE-- WITH ALL THE VILLAGES. FROM THE SHELL PEOPLE OF THE WEST TO THE BONE TALKERS OF THE EAST.
HE WILL CARRY THEM ALL INTO TOMORROW-- ON HIS BACK IF NEED BE.
THEY NEED A LEADER. IF ONLY FOR A LITTLE WHILE.

SHALIM WILL WAIT FOR HIM. SHALIM WILL UNDERST--

NO!

WHY ARE THEY DOING THIS?!
HE HAS BROUGHT *GIFTS!* HE *IS* A GIFT!
SKLICH!
SKLICH!
SKLICH!

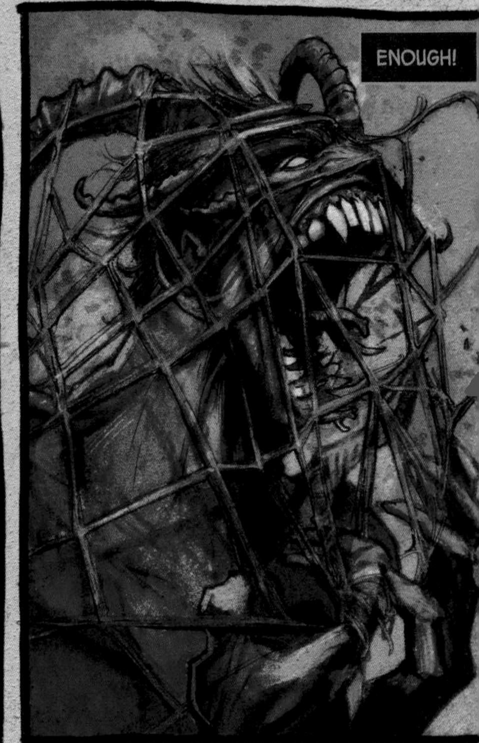

ENOUGH!

THEN THERE IS A SOFT WHICKERING ON THE WIND, AND HE KNOWS ALL IS LOST.

THUNNNK!!!
THE DOOR IS LIGHTER THIS TIME.

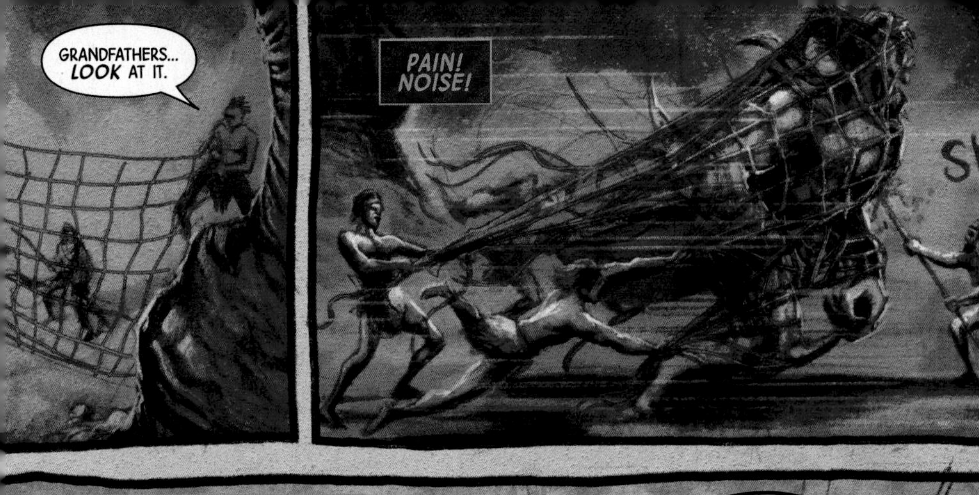

GRANDFATHERS... LOOK AT IT.
PAIN! NOISE!
SHLUK!

TAMMUZ IS CHANGED, BUT THESE ARE STILL *HIS PEOPLE.* HE NEED ONLY EXPLAIN, AND ALL WILL BE WELL.

GLK! HRAAAGGH!!!

HE TRIES TO WREST WORDS FROM HIS LUNGS, BUT HIS THROAT GRINDS THEM INTO CHAFF.

KRA-KOOMMM

PERHAPS YOU'RE NOT SUCH A MILKSOP AFTER ALL, EH, SHALIM?

... THAT BIRTHMARK...

TAMMUZ?

WH... WHERE AM I?

YOU BEAR MY MARK

NO.

THERE WAS *ANOTHER.*

I TURN MY FACE TOWARD YOU

THEY HAVE ALL TURNED THEIRS FROM ME. EVEN SHALIM.

I WOULD HAVE GIVEN THEM *EVERYTHING.*

I AM THE ONE BELOW ALL

WITH THESE HANDS I BREAK

WITH THIS MOUTH I HOWL

BREAK. YES, I THINK I WOULD LIKE TO BREAK THINGS NOW.

I WOULD LIKE THAT VERY MUCH.

ITS LIVER, SHALIM! LOOK AT IT!
YOU EARNED IT. EAT YOUR FILL.
...
LATER, PERHAPS.
FRIENDS!
LOOK AT US!
BELLIES FULL OF MEAT...
GREASE DRIPPING DOWN OUR CHINS...
ALL IS AS IT SHOULD BE.
ALMOST.
FIRST, LET US HAIL THE TRUE AIM OF MY SON, SHALIM!
THE POOR CREATURE WAS FRANTIC WITH PAIN, AND HE SHOWED IT A HUNTER'S MERCY.

BUT WHILE OUR SPEARS AND ARROWS FELLED THE BRUTE, THEY DID NOT SUMMON IT.
IT WAS THE MOTHER GODDESS' GIFT!
BY NOW YOU WILL ALL HAVE REALIZED THAT SOMEONE IS MISSING FROM THIS FEAST...
TAMMUZ. DEAR TAMMUZ.
MY SISTER TOOK HIM IN WHEN THE FEVER TOOK HIS MOTHER. HE WAS FAMILY.
TODAY HE OFFERED HIMSELF WILLINGLY TO THE MOTHER GODDESS' GOOD GREEN EYE.
I KNOW THIS BECAUSE I WAS WITH HIM AT THE END.
SHLORPP
HE BEGGED ME TO TELL YOU NOT TO MOURN HIM.
"HE CROSSED OVER WITH A SMILING HEART BECAUSE HE KNEW HIS PEOPLE'S FUTURE WAS ASSURED."

THERE HAS BEEN SOME TALK--ESPECIALLY AMONG THE YOUNG--OF ABANDONING OUR LANDS...
OF FORAGING IN THE WETLANDS LIKE OUR HALF-WILD ANCESTORS.
BUT LOOK! THIS MEAT IS A BOON FROM THE MOTHER GODDESS HERSELF!
IT IS PROOF THAT WE CAN KEEP FAITH WITH OUR WAYS AND STILL HAVE ALL WE NEED!
TAMMUZ HAS SHOWN US THE PRICE THE EYE DEMANDS. IT IS THE PRICE OF CIVILIZATION.
BUT WE NEED NOT PAY IT OURSELVES!
TOMORROW I WILL TAKE A HUNTING PARTY TO THE VILLAGE OF THE BONE TALKERS.
FATHER...
WE WILL--NN!--SURPRISE THEM. WE WILL SUBDUE THEM, AND WE WILL OFFER THEM UP TO THE GOOD GREEN EYE.
AND WE WILL BE MADE WHOLE.
A-DAD!
A-DAD!
A-DAD!
FATHER, ITS EYE!

WAIT. I FEEL... GLLKKK!!!
THE FIRE GUTTERS.
ADAD, WHAT IS-- HALCCHH!!!
THE CHEERING STOPS.
THERE IS RIPPING. THERE IS PAIN. THE FEAST IS OVER.
GOOD. PERHAPS NOW THEY WILL UNDERSTAND.
THE GREEN DOOR OPENS LIKE A FLOWER.
NO!
HE IS RETURNED.

WITH A THOUGHT, HE SUMMONS HIMSELF TO HIMSELF...AND SMILES.
THE POWER FEELS DIFFERENT THIS TIME. IT IS NOT MEANT FOR BUILDING.
HIS GOOD GREEN EYE WIDENS, DRINKING IN EVERY DELECTABLE TWITCH AND SHUDDER OF HIS MURDERERS' BODIES...
...UNTIL ONLY ONE REMAINS.
I...I DIDN'T KNOW, TAMMUZ! I SWEAR!

TAMMUZ KNOWS HE COULD SPEAK NOW IF HE WISHED--SHAPE THE ROCKSLIDE IN HIS CHEST INTO WORDS.
SPEAK THE WHY OF IT. TEACH THE LESSON OF IT.
HE COULD STILL LEAVE WITH SHALIM AS THEY PLANNED. EVEN NOW--EVEN AFTER THE SCREAMS AND THE RENDING--IT MIGHT NOT BE TOO LATE.
THEY COULD STILL FIND THAT BETTER PLACE IN HIS MIND.
HE COULD STOP.

HE COULD STOP MAKING THEM PAY.

IF HE WISHED.

SHLKK

BUT THERE IS A VOICE OF GREEN FIRE IN HIS HEAD, FROM A PLACE BELOW ALL PLACES.

A VOICE THAT SAYS "NEVER."

AND WHEN TAMMUZ FINALLY LEAVES THE VILLAGE...
...HE LEAVES ALONE.

TIME OF MONSTERS

ALEX PAKNADEL & AL EWING STORY ALEX PAKNADEL SCRIPT JUAN FERREYRA ART & COVER VC'S CORY PETIT LETTERER

RON LIM & RACHELLE ROSENBERG VARIANT COVER ARTISTS PROFESSOR NATALIE MUNRO & DR. STEPHEN CURTIS SPECIAL THANKS

WIL MOSS & SARAH BRUNSTAD EDITORS TOM BREVOORT EXECUTIVE EDITOR C.B. CEBULSKI EDITOR IN CHIEF

HULK CREATED BY STAN LEE & JACK KIRBY

VALERIO SCHITI & JASON KEITH
DEFENDERS: THE BEST DEFENSE VARIANT

SKOTTIE YOUNG
DEFENDERS: THE BEST DEFENSE VARIANT

SAL BUSCEMA & DAVE McCAIG
DEFENDERS: THE BEST DEFENSE HIDDEN GEM VARIANT

Lee InHyuk

DANIEL WARREN JOHNSON & MIKE SPICER
IMMORTAL SHE-HULK VARIANT

ALEX ROSS
IMMORTAL SHE-HULK TIMELESS VARIANT

SIMONE DI MEO
IMMORTAL SHE-HULK EMPYRE VARIANT

JOE BENNETT, RUY JOSÉ & PAUL MOUNTS